D1548845

The Al-Hamlet Summ
Sulayman Al-Bassam

Original playscript in English and Arabic
with an Introduction by Graham Holderness

"The writing is electrifying ... so relevant to the nightmare that is brewing in the Middle East ... so vivid and eloquent in the theatrical means it uses to confront it." The Scotsman

The Al-Hamlet Summit is a loose adaptation of Shakespeare's Hamlet and a remarkable piece of 21st century theatre set in the cauldron of Middle Eastern discontent.

Having gained control of a modern Arab state, a ruthless dictator attempts a westernised experiment in thrall to arms dealers and propped up by U.S. dollars. Yet a catastrophic war is brewing, he is besieged by enemy neighbours from without and a growing Islamic extremism from within, whilst his predecessor's son, Hamlet, is plotting revenge.

Al-Bassam's Summit is Hamlet boldly re-imagined as pure, deadly politics.

"A superbly constructed dramatisation of a society's descent into fundamentalism and chaos." Sunday Herald

This edition is illustrated throughout with performance stills from Al-Bassam's internationally award-winning 2004 production of the play.

Sulayman Al-Bassam was born in Kuwait in 1972. Other works include The Mirror for Princes, an imaginative exploration of the current war in Iraq as seen from the viewpoint of an 8th century Abbasid scribe (2006). His Arabic version of Richard III premieres in 2007 as part of The R.S.C.'s Complete Works Festival. He lives between Kuwait and London.

Professor Graham Holderness is author of numerous critical studies in Renaissance and modern theatre.

Sulayman Al-Bassam

For my parents, with all my love

The Al-Hamlet Summit

A political arabesque

The Al-Hamlet Summit

A political arabesque

BY SULAYMAN AL-BASSAM
with an Introduction by Graham Holderness

UNIVERSITY OF HERTFORDSHIRE PRESS

First published in Great Britain in 2006 by
University of Hertfordshire Press
University of Hertfordshire
College Lane
Hatfield
Hertfordshire AL10 9AB

British Library Cataloguing in Publication Data
A catalogue record for this book is available from the British Library

ISBN 1-902806-62-X

Design by Geoff Green Book Design, CB4 5RA
Cover design by John Robertshaw, AL5 2JB
Printed in Great Britain by Antony Rowe Ltd, SN14 6LH

English cover photograph © Stephanie Kulbach
Author photograph on page 1 © Ben Boorman
Photographs on pages 49, 53, 59, 65, 72, 79 and 83 © Arne Magnussen

Contents

Introduction

✛|✛
✛|✛

GRAHAM HOLDERNESS

1

Shakespeare touched the Arab world astonishingly early. In 1608, during the 3rd voyage of the East India Company, on the island of Socotra, at the entry to the Gulf of Aden, the crew of the *Red Dragon* staged a performance of *Hamlet*, a play then less than a decade old, and published only 5 years previously. The ship's captain William Keeling obviously shared Shakespearean interests with his patron (and major East India Company member) the Earl of Southampton (see Holderness and Loughrey, 'Arabesque', 2006).

Socotra is now an integral part of the Arab Republic of Yemen; and *Hamlet*, of course, needs no introduction. Shortly after the First World War, F.S. Boas conferred on the English Merchant Navy 'the proud distinction of having been the pioneer in carrying Shakespearean drama to the uttermost ends of the earth' (Boas, p. 95). Yemen no longer seems quite so distant from the United Kingdom, but this example of *Hamlet* exported to the Middle East, by agents of a nascent British Empire, certainly confirms Michael Neill's judgement that Shakespeare's plays were 'entangled from the beginning with the projects of nation-building, empire and colonization' (Neill, p. 168).

2

Shakespeare re-entered the Arab world in the late 19th century as theatre: that is, the plays were translated and adapted specifically to form the repertoire of dramatic companies in Egypt and other Arab countries. *Hamlet* was first performed in Egypt around 1893, and was immediately popular with local audiences, who had a strong taste for ghosts, revenge and madness. Productions were based on translations derived from 18th-century French versions of Shakespeare. Hence, the play was radically adapted, with whole scenes deleted and songs introduced; with Hamlet making love to Ophelia in the language of Arab love poetry, and with all obscenity discreetly purged. Above all, the play was converted from Shakespeare's tragedy into a historical romance, in which Hamlet defeats his uncle, ascends the throne, and reigns with the Ghost's blessing: 'may you live a joyful life on earth, pardoned in heaven' (translation by Tanius 'Abdoh, quoted by Al-Shetawi, p. 44). The 'happy ending' Hamlet of the French versions, although clearly shaped by Enlightenment views of Shakespeare, were actually more faithful to the story of Amleth in Saxo Grammaticus than was the Shakespearean tragedy, just as Nahum Tate's notorious happy-ending King Lear restored the Lear-tale to its original romance form. In Egypt in the late 19th and early 20th centuries, Hamlet flourished as a stage show, independently of textual scholarship, and appeared in radically revised, rewritten, and reconstructed adaptations. Early Arab Shakespeare shared this wide liberty of adaptation with the Restoration and 18th-century theatres, where (as David Scott Kastan puts it):

> On the stage... Shakespeare was not merely modernized, but aggressively modified to satisfy the expectations of the fashionable audiences that filled the theatres... turned... into a contemporary playwright, at once modern and highbrow, for the theatrical environment in which he was now performed... (Kastan, p. 14).

This ungenerous view of the Restoration theatre is echoed in Mahmoud Al-Shetawi's harsh judgement of early Arab Shakespeare: 'Overall, the early stage productions of Hamlet were crude, vulgarizing Shakespeare's masterpiece in order to please the illiterate audience' (Al-Shetawi, p. 46). Alexander Pope said much the same of the Lord Chamberlain's Men. Free adaptation from French models continued to be the norm in Arab cultures: the translation of Hamlet made by Khalil Mutran from the French (1916), in which Hamlet kills Claudius and ascends the throne, remained popular in Egypt for many years.

Shakespeare's absorption into Middle Eastern culture was not, by any means, a simple process of imperialist transmission and passive colonial reception. 'Shakespeare,' wrote Nadia Al-Bahar, 'was transplanted into Arab soil' (Al-Bahar, p. 13). 'Transplanted' indicates not a simple exchange but a cross-cultural migration across borders, in which the artefact becomes rooted in different soil, and there adapts itself to the local climate and conditions. *Hamlet* has been 'assimilated', said Al-Shetawi, thoroughly woven into the 'fabric of Arab creative processes' (p. 60).

Hamlet was continuously produced, in several different translations, in Egypt from the late 19th century onwards. On the other hand, this performance tradition did not produce a consistent 'Arab' interpretation of *Hamlet*. 'The play,' writes Al-Shetawi, 'has always been known to the Arab audience and frequently staged in the Arab world'; but it has also 'always been adapted to suit the conditions of local Arab theatres and native culture'. Appropriations have, for example, been sharply divided between heroic and anti-heroic Hamlets:

> With the exception of early productions... Hamlet has always been viewed as a romantic hero who sets out to fight corruption and dies for the cause of justice... Other Arabic productions of *Hamlet* present Hamlet as an Arab intellectual, impotent to cope with the realities of his society (Al-Shetawi, p. 49).

Margaret Litvin addresses this contradiction in Arab Shakespeare between Hamlet the hero and Hamlet the intellectual, and posits a chronological break in the tradition of Arabic appropriations of *Hamlet* some time in the late 1970s. Hamlet the romantic freedom fighter of the post-colonial tradition gave way to a series of Hamlets disarmed, impotent and emotionally crippled by the weight of their destiny:

> Collapsing into incoherence and tears at crucial moments; listening in silence as other characters claim their best lines; leaving their soliloquies to be read posthumously by gravediggers; or finding no hearers but the deaf and the dead (Litvin 2005).

Litvin cites productions and adaptations from Egypt, Syria and Tunisia to demonstrate this reorientation: *Hamlet wakes Up Late* (Syria 1976); *A Theatre Company Found a Theatre and Dramatized* Hamlet (Tunisia and Jordan 1984); *Dance of the Scorpions* (Egypt 1989); *Forget Hamlet/Ophelia's Window* (performed Egypt 1994, published Beirut). All these plays deploy technical devices to challenge the norms of conventional theatrical representation; all are sceptical about the power of words to achieve change. Claudius is invariably the powerful Arab despot, while Hamlet is the 'Arab intellectual, a figure who is commonly portrayed as impotent when it comes to responding positively to the miserable conditions of his country' (Al-Shetawi, p. 48).

3

This complex tradition was one of the starting-points for Sulayman Al-Bassam's The Al-Hamlet Summit, first performed in English in August 2002 as part of the Edinburgh International Fringe Festival, where it was awarded the Fringe First Award for excellence and innovation in writing and directing. It was subsequently presented, in September 2002, at the 14th Cairo International Festival of Experimental Theatre, where it won Best Production and Best Director Awards. As a result of a Japanese commission, the play moved into the Arabic language and undertook a world tour. It has played at the Riverside Studios in London (March 2004), the Singapore International Arts Festival (June 2005), at Elsinore Castle in Denmark (August 2005), and at other festival venues across the globe (Seoul, Tokyo, Warsaw, Tehran).

From 2001 onwards, the work had been through various adaptations of the Shakespeare text, performed by the Zaoum Theatre Company: Hamlet in Kuwait, performed in Kuwait (2001), and The Arab League Hamlet, performed at a festival in Tunisia (2001). The earlier versions were both adaptations of the Shakespearean text. By contrast, The Al-Hamlet Summit jettisoned Shakespeare's language and rewrote Hamlet into modern English, which attempts a concrete and objective translation of Arabic concepts and rhetoric into English, producing what the author called a 'cross-cultural construction' (Al-Bassam 2003). Al-Bassam produced and directed versions in both Arabic and English. This edition makes available a definitive text of The Al-Hamlet Summit in both English and Arabic.

Al-Bassam's play maps a Middle Eastern political tragedy onto the template of Shakespeare's Hamlet. The key characters carry Shakespearean names, and occupy parallel situations within their own modern Middle Eastern world. Hamlet's father, the old ruler, has been poisoned, and his position usurped by his brother Claudius, who bears more than a passing resemblance to Saddam Hussein. Gertrude, Ophelia, Polonius and Laertes all play roles comparable to those of their Shakespearean namesakes, but redomesticated into an

Islamic Arab context. The regime is threatened, as Denmark is threatened at the beginning of Hamlet, by Fortinbras's troops lining the borders, and internally by the 'People's Liberation Brigade', which has been distributing leaflets claiming Old Hamlet was assassinated. Where Claudius in Shakespeare's play resolves the Norwegian threat by diplomacy, Claudius in Al-Hamlet responds with violence and atrocity:

> **Polonius:** I've got 300 men working round the clock gathering up the leaflets.
>
> **Claudius:** Forget the leaflets, burn the townships, all of them – I want them all burnt by dawn (p. 37).

Fortinbras's army is backed by the West, 'armed with millions of dollars of foreign equipment'. Behind the suggestions of foreign intervention lies the West's greed for Arab oil (Claudius is obsessively concerned to protect the pipelines from sabotage).

In a scene which is the equivalent of Hamlet 3.3, instead of displaying remorse and praying for forgiveness, Claudius voices what is virtually a religion of oil and dollars:

> Oh God: Petro dollars. Teach me the meaning of petro dollars.
>
> I have no other God than you, I am created in your image, I seek guidance from you the All Seeing, the All Knowing Master of Worlds, Prosperity and Order (p. 70).

At the end of the play Fortinbras clearly intends to sustain this policy and this faith: 'It won't be easy, terrorism is not yet defeated, but the pipeline will be completed within a year' (p.85).

The West appears in the play in the shadowy persona of the Arms Dealer, who spoke English in the Arabic version, and was played by a woman in the English version. The Arms Dealer converses with, and supplies arms to Hamlet, Ophelia, Claudius, Gertrude and, finally, Fortinbras. S/he will provide weapons to anyone prepared to pay, even if s/he is arming opponents. S/he remains in place at the end: 'Arms Dealer enters and walks towards Fortinbras incredibly slowly.' (p. 86).

Just as in Hamlet, Claudius recognises that the real enemy of his regime lies within, so Claudius and Polonius in The Al-Hamlet Summit are vigilant against signs of domestic subversion. Opposition and dissent are read as fundamentalist terrorism. Polonius sees in Hamlet's letters to Ophelia the 'apocalyptic imagery', the 'yearning for violent and comprehensive change to the world order' that is naturally linked with 'terrorist activities'. Both Hamlet and Ophelia become Islamicised, adopting traditional Muslim costume; and both become, from the perspective of the ruling regime, 'terrorists'. Ophelia is associated, as Yvette K. Khoury has observed, with the Palestinian cause (Khoury 2005), and dies as a suicide bomber; Hamlet (who adopts *'a short white thowb, with a long beard'* [p. 81]) shoots Polonius, and at the end of the play is seen leading the liberation army.

> **Claudius:** Just two hours ago, our forces began an attack on terrorist positions belonging to Hamlet and his army. These continue as I speak. This conflict began when Hamlet laid siege to our democracy, our values and our people through a brutal series of kidnappings and terrorist bombings that have killed many innocent victims and shocked the world community (p. 84).

The equation between Islamic fundamentalist and terrorist militant is one that Hamlet internalises. This is the equivalent of both Hamlet's revenge and his madness, a vindictive fantasy bloodbath that deliberately echoes (or even parodies) the language of the Holy Koran:

> I bear witness that there is no God but Allah and that Mohammad is his messenger... I will clean this land, I will make it pure, I understand, I do understand, but I will cleanse it for you, I will prepare it for your return, even if it costs me my life, I will clean it, I will purge it, blood will flow, I will make blood flow in torrents, I swear in my father's name, I swear in the name of Allah... (p. 82, p. 61).

4

Where does this adaptation sit vis-à-vis both Arab Shakespeare and dominant theatrical interpretations of the play in the West? Margaret Litvin argues that Al-Bassam has discarded the impotent intellectual Hamlets of the late 20th century and re-established a link with the romantic figure that had dominated earlier performances of *Hamlet* in the Arab theatre. Al-Bassam's Hamlet is 'not the fractured non-protagonist of recent Arab plays but rather recalls... the hero Hamlets of the 1960s and 1970s' (Litvin 2005). In this analysis, Al-Bassam has by-passed the previous two decades, and reconnected with an older

Arabic tradition. The *Al-Hamlet Summit* is divided into sections corresponding to the Islamic times of prayer, which seems to echo Riyad 'Ismat's 1973 Damascus production, where the play was divided into three parts – *huzn* (sorrow), *al-thawra* (rebellion), *al-shahadah* (martyrdom) (see Al-Shetawi, p 48).

On the other hand, the figure of the Islamic militant, which Al-Bassam's Hamlet grows to resemble, cannot be so easily identified with the heroes of a previous century, although he is certainly an active crusader against corruption and a militant for justice:

Hamlet: The real enemy is here, in the palace, amongst us.

Laertes: There will be no nation to fight over unless we defeat Fortinbras.

Hamlet: We'll have no nation to lose unless we destroy the rot that devours it from within (p. 58).

Hamlet becomes wholly the man of action, rejecting language and the intellect, committing himself unequivocally to violence:

Hamlet: ... the time for the pen has passed and we enter the era of the sword... No more words... words are dead, they died on our tongues, council is the weakest form of faith, now we must mouth meaning with our flesh (p. 82).

Conversely, although Hamlet's death is a significant gesture of martyrdom ('I do not approximate God/I come closer to him/in giving of myself'), it is only one detail in the final scene of universal carnage, where a failed coup-d'etat, the converging of Western power and Fortinbras's assumption of authority are all presented with the excited objectivity of a media event. If Hamlet does 'clean this land' it is only to create an empty space into which Fortinbras can move his troops. Islamic militancy has not provided a solution, only a dramatic denouement:

Fortinbras: I have biblical claims upon this land, it is empty and barren and my presence here is a fact that has not been invented (p. 85).

5

Insofar as there was a separate, local Arab tradition of adapting and appropriating Shakespeare, Al-Bassam's work is obviously part of it.

But by writing in English, Al-Bassam has chosen to work partially inside an Anglophone culture (or set of cultures), which is, as Michael Neill phrases it, 'saturated with Shakespeare': 'Our ways of thinking about such basic issues as nationality, gender and racial difference are inescapably inflected by his writing' (Neill, p. 184). Al-Bassam has explicitly confirmed that the work is 'cross-cultural', speaking from an Arab perspective but also to an English-speaking audience.

> The script was written from a contemporary Arab perspective. It carries many concerns and issues of today's Arab world and its relationship to the West. At the same time, it addresses these concerns to an English-speaking audience. The cross-cultural construction of the piece creates a sense of implication in the affairs of the other (Dent 2003).

This sounds like the cultural 'hybridity' that occurs when an imperial discourse penetrates a post-colonial culture and merges with local and native materials to produce a synthetic fusion. But The Al-Hamlet Summit does not fit so easily into this or any of the available models provided by post-colonial criticism. Any writer who so deliberately places his work on a cultural or national margin, or looks to work across territorial and historical borders, is seeking a difficult and precarious balance, and is likely to find himself challenged from all sides, as Al-Bassam himself confirms:

> For some The Al-Hamlet Summit was the work of a Westernised traitor that falsely approximated between Islam and the propagation of violence. For others, and I'm happy to say the majority and particularly the young, The Al-Hamlet Summit gave vital and much-needed expression to today's Arab concerns and presented them to the West in a sophisticated and human form (Al-Bassam 2003, p. 86).

Even Al-Bassam's admirers have found themselves questioning his position. Peter J. Smith (2004) asks:

> Is it not the case that the portrayal of Hamlet and Ophelia as Muslim fundamentalists and suicide bombers will have the effect of exacerbating – even promoting – the racist assumptions typified by the tabloid press? (Smith, pp. 74–5).

But then Smith questions his own authority to make such judgements: 'Who am I as a non-Muslim, non-Arabic speaking Englishman to tell Sulayman Al-Bassam how to write and direct his adaptation?' (Smith,

p. 75). Margaret Litvin raises similar questions about Al-Bassam's 'metropolitan perspective':

> The play does not engage with the actual history of Arabic Shakespeare... In positioning himself as writing not to but on behalf of Arab audiences, he also washes out the differences between... personal and local backgrounds... Al-Bassam did not set out to write a *Hamlet* play for an Arab audience. Rather he sought to shock and implicate his Western, mainly British, audience by recreating the 'voyeuristic thrill' and the 'sense of strangeness in familiarity' that Arab audiences got from his earlier productions (Litvin 2005).

Al-Bassam is planning to develop the play into a TV film for Arab audiences, so this judgement may in due course need revising. However, these critical responses are all testimony to *The Al-Hamlet Summit*'s capacity to generate dialogue across borders, dialogue that challenges and questions and enters reservations, but remains fundamentally an international conversation. As such, it offers an alternative, an urgently imperative alternative, to mutual misunderstanding and reciprocal violence. What Al-Bassam called the 'cultural symbiosis' manifest in the play was clearly designed to form a ground for dialogue (not necessarily comfortable or unchallenging) between East and West. The move from the earlier versions, which were adaptations of the Shakespeare text, to a more contemporary form, which allowed for the fuller expression of Arab experience, was clearly critical in this process.

6

The writing of *The Al-Hamlet Summit* began with the experience of globalisation:

> I was in Cairo with an exiled Iraqi theatre director and a Palestinian theatre troupe from Ramallah drinking coffee in the bazaar when a boy came running past us, chanting: 'Al-Kull murtabit/Am-reeca qarabit' ('Everything is linked/America just got closer...'). It was September the 11th and news from New York was just beginning to stream across the television screens. In all the confusion of that night, I remember the words of one of the Palestinian actors: 'The hell in New York today will bring hell to Ramallah tomorrow' (Al-Bassam 2003, p. 85).

9/11 is the supreme instance of globalisation, viewed here from a range of different perspectives. The boy's chant seems to celebrate with a certain triumphalism the shrinking globe and the ease with which Islamic terrorism can reach to the very heart of America's political and economic institutions. The Palestinian actor thinks ruefully of the consequences, immediate reprisal not from America but from Israel, and against the Palestinians. Global events know no barriers of time and space.

In an article on 9/11 British Prime Minister Tony Blair echoed these sentiments exactly. 9/11 'brought home the true meaning of globalisation':

> In this globalised world, once chaos and strife have got a grip on a region or a country, trouble is soon exported... It was, after all, a dismal camp in the foothills of Afghanistan that gave birth to the murderous assault on the sparkling heart of New York's financial centre (Blair, p. 119).

This is the negative side of globalisation. But, from Blair's perspective, globalisation also provides the potential solution to such problems. Blair reflects that the West can 'use the power of community to bring the benefits of globalisation to all' (p. 121) in the form of truly universal values: 'values of liberty, the rule of law, human rights and a pluralist society... Values that are "universal and worthy of respect in every culture"' (p. 121). The vehicle for disseminating these values globally is economic penetration: increased trade flows, and greater involvement of the private sector in public finance (p. 122).

Al-Bassam clearly intended The Al-Hamlet Summit as an intervention into this fraught conversation:

> The globalisation of politics is deceptive. Every Arab knows that George Bush said 'either you are with us or you are against us' and everyone in the West now knows that Saddam is bad. This is globalisation of politics, but it does very little to increase dialogue between cultures. All it does is promote vacuous 'world views'. This is where culture and theatre become vital. They permit complexity and difference and they permit the weak to be other than pitied and the cruel to be other than hated. Theatre challenges the accepted world views and breaks the mirrors of authority. Shakespeare understood that power very well (Dent 2003).

Globalisation is not only inevitable but desirable, since it is the only route to mutual understanding and a stable world. Everything really is linked, as the Arab boy recognised. The problem is how to develop those links without conflict and violence; without the supremacy of the West; without the suppression of alternative cultures and consequent global homogenisation. In this process theatre has a critical role to play:

> The events of 9-11 and the political fallout since have drawn to light the inextricable intertwining of the fates of Arab peoples and those of the West.
> Everything is linked and the much-touted 'clash of civilizations' simplifies and tries to obscure what is a complex series of overlapping and interpenetrating cultural realities that are tied together in fatal symbiosis (Al-Bassam 2003, p. 85).

This is quite a different approach from Tony Blair's vision of a universalisation of enlightenment values of liberal democracy via the spread of free-market capitalism. Although he does not speak for Islamic fundamentalism or terrorist violence, Al-Bassam shows them as the inevitable consequences of an alliance between native Arab despotism and the economic machinations of the West. In Shakespeare, Hamlet is driven reluctantly towards revenge, and in The Al-Hamlet Summit Hamlet and Ophelia seem to have no option but the bloody and suicidal course they undertake.

7

Between 1608, when, from the deck of the Red Dragon, Shakespeare's lines echoed emptily around the Arab world, and 2002, when Al-Bassam's adaptation found a common acceptance across both East and West, empires rose and fell. But one thing changed. In 1608 Shakespeare was virtually talking to himself. In 2002 Shakespeare was the substance of a global conversation. 'Everything is linked' in the globalised world, either through violence or through an acceptance of reciprocal 'implication'. The Al-Hamlet Summit opens a conversation over the ground of our reconciliation.

Introduction – Works cited

I am very grateful to Margaret Litvin, Yvette K. Khoury, Peter J. Smith, Bryan Loughrey and Sulayman Al-Bassam for providing material used in the writing of this introduction.

Al-Bahar, Nadia, 1976. 'Shakespeare in Early Arabic Adaptations', *Shakespeare Translation*, 3, 13–25.

Al-Bassam, Sulayman, 2003. 'Introduction to the publication of *The Al-Hamlet Summit*' in *Theatre Forum Magazine*, 22 (Winter/Spring), 85–8.

Al-Shetawi, Mahmoud, 1999. 'Hamlet in Arabic', *Journal of Intercultural Studies*, vol. 20, no. 1, 43–96.

Blair, Tony, 2002. 'The Power of World Community', in Mark Leonard, ed. *Re-Ordering the World*. London: Foreign Policy Centre, 119–24.

Boas, Frederick S., 1923. *Shakespeare and the Universities and Other Studies in Elizabethan Drama*. New York: Appleton.

Dent, Shirley, 2003. 'Interview: Sulayman Al-Bassam', *Culture Wars*. N.p. [Available at <http://www.culturewars.org.uk/2003–01/albassam.htm>] [Accessed 11 November 2005].

Holderness, Graham and Bryan Loughrey, 2006. 'Arabesque: Shakespeare and Globalisation', *Globalisation and its Discontents: Writing the Global Culture*. London: Boydell and Brewer, 36–96.

Kastan, David Scott, 1999. *Shakespeare After Theory*. London: Routledge.

Khoury, Yvette K., 2005. '"Glaring Stare": Middle Eastern Presentation of Ophelia'. Paper presented to the Modern Language Association, 2005 Annual Convention, seminar on 'Gender in Arabic Interpretations of Shakespeare', Washington DC.

Litvin, Margaret, 2005. 'Sulayman Al-Bassam's *Al-Hamlet Summit* in the Arab *Hamlet* Tradition'. Paper presented to the American

Comparative Literature Association, 2005 Annual Meeting, Pennsylvania State University.

Loomba, Ania and Martin Orkin, eds, 1998. *Post-colonial Shakespeares*. London: Routledge.

Neill, Michael, 1998. 'Postcolonial Shakespeare? Writing away from the centre', in Loomba and Orkin (1998), 164–85.

Smith, Peter J., 2004. 'Sulayman Al-Bassam's *The Al-Hamlet Summit* in an Age of Terrorism'. *Shakespeare Bulletin*, 22:4, 65–78.

Author's note

On *the road with* The Al-Hamlet Summit

Gertrude: Beirut?
Polonius: Too many militias.
Gertrude: Damascus?
Claudius: Too many thinkers.
Polonius: Cairo?
Gertrude: Too many liars. Sana'a?
[...]
Claudius: London?
Polonius and Gertrude: London!!

Before almost each performance of the piece in Arabic, this string of capital cities and their corresponding epithets that plays out in Act Three, underwent last-minute changes in the wings of the stage, depending on which Arab ambassadors were in the audience that night who, it was feared, would take mortal offence at the impudence of these powdered fops!

Satire, it seems, wins hands down over tragedy or political theatre as a breeding ground for diplomatic scandal. The idea of theatre-makers self-censoring their material to avoid offending nationalist sentiment appears, perhaps, risible to a Western reader. But in the Arab world, this is no joke!

Snow in Iran

One of the overriding images that remain in my mind of the presentation of *The Al-Hamlet Summit* in the Middle East was on a snowy night in Tehran. Less than an hour before the scheduled opening performance, I was informed that the play had to be presented to the censor. I had been expecting this, but over five hundred people had already gathered outside the main theatre in Tehran, and were waiting impatiently for the doors to open. Performing for the censor would mean they would wait in the snow for two hours more. The festival organisers duly made their apologies to the five hundred snowmen and we proceeded to perform the entire piece to rows and rows of empty seats, in the midst of which sat one turbaned cleric.

Costumes had already been sewn to prevent female calves showing, Ophelia and Gertrude had already practised emoting with headscarves; but the censor took issue with the use of the verse from the Holy Koran that bellows out (in Act Four) to prevent Hamlet from emptying his gun into his mother's womb. We proceeded to have a most civilised debate over the meaning and use of this 'holy' signifier. I explained that of all the impressions generated by an audience about the relationship between Islam and violence, this moment was, incontestably, the most clear and definite example of Islam's condemnation of violence. The cleric, a soft-spoken and intelligent man, eventually gave a small nod and the audience entered in throngs, tapping the snow from their shoulders.

'Riot, old chap? Is there a back door?'
In Cairo, we performed in a small theatre. A large crowd had gathered, attracted by what had been billed as a political bombshell. Tickets ran scarce, and large queues started to form. The arrival of ten foreign jury members accompanied by their ten translators, followed by a cortege of Mercedes delivering a Western ambassador and his guests, set alight rumours that the play was a private imperialist jig. A riot ensued, the crowds tried to break down the glass doors of the theatre. Police were called and seven people arrested. Meanwhile the ambassador was whisked away through the stage door. To calm ruffled nerves we were asked by the festival organisers to make a command performance again at midnight. The crowds duly returned and the show began again: it was the best performance of the *Summit* in English to date.

The Grand Masquerade

I was once accused by an Arab theatre critic in a public debate in Kuwait of receiving funding for *The Al-Hamlet Summit* from a covert Israeli organisation that was masquerading as a Japanese funding body that sought to promote an Anti-Arab agenda masquerading inside a World Classic; and – wonder of wonders – these shady masters of conspiracy commissioned the piece in Arabic in order that it better masquerade as an authentic piece of Arab theatre.

⌗ Fortinbras's self-censorship of the word 'Israel' in the dying moments of the play should be played with great delicacy. The censorship of this signifier and its interruption is crucial to its meaning. This is not a play about Israeli-Arab issues and it would be wrong for the meaning of the piece to be hijacked in that way. Equally, however, one cannot explore cycles of violence in the Middle East region without including Israel in the equation. When faced with the knot of problems that constitute contemporary Middle Eastern politics, audiences (particularly in the West) have a tendency to take their cue from Fortinbras's speech and say: "Ah! That is what the author meant!" This allows them off the hook; whereas the real intention of Fortinbras's speech is to prevent any kind of moral closure. This absence of moral closure is also the absence of authorial judgement; it leaves the spectator in a kind of moral free-fall, which is empowering to an audience.

⌗ I see no reason why the play should necessarily have to perform in a summit setting with tables, chairs, red carpets, microphones and little bottles of mineral water. One can imagine it unfolding with equal dramatic plausibility in an entirely empty space.

⌗ The Empty Space that Hamlet refers to in his monologue in Act Three has its origins in the architectural shape of the *Majlis* (a primarily male gathering parlour common across Gulf Arab houses). In the Majlis, seating is arranged around the edges of the room, leaving an entirely empty central area in the middle. The architecture of the Security Council meeting room in New York is similar, only circular.

⌗ Religious dogma invades the piece from all sides. It is the mask of the ruler, the battle cry of the oppressed and the strategy of the revolutionary. Doubt and debate are hounded out of existence.

⌗ Act One is a series of events in one day. Beyond that, time in the play remains largely consecutive and fluid, with some compressions and accelerations of time entering in Acts Four and Five. The names of the Acts, therefore, which are the names of the five daily prayers in Islam, are indicators of mood, rather than specific indicators of time.

⌗ Current political events – and our perceptions of them – hang like a misty landscape, half-perceived, in the backdrop of the play.

⌗ The Arms Dealer is a ghost, companion, grave-digger, man, woman or child.

⌗ I write in English. However, the process of generating the Arabic performance of the text also ended up impacting on the original English text. This can be seen, for instance, with Hamlet's 'Peace be upon the Grave Dwellers' monologue, and the 'Horse of War' skit in the middle of the play. These episodes are, perhaps more than others, culturally specific in the sense that they draw upon and echo a uniquely Arab-specific set of signifiers. The 'Grave Dwellers' speech echoes the words of the Prophet Muhammed (Peace Be Upon Him) in his last days, whilst the 'Horse of War' scene acts as a parody on a specifically Arab penchant for glorifying the past.

⌗ There are also some culturally significant differences between the English and Arabic texts presented here. Noticeably, in Claudius's 'Petro Dollars' monologue where the English reads: 'Oh God: Petro dollars. Teach me the meaning of petro dollars', the Arabic text reads: 'Oh God, *God of Money* teach me the meaning of petro dollars'. The English text inscribes itself in a secular linguistic universe. The Arabic text works within a theistic signifying order.

⌗ The Arabic translation of the work was made by many hands, and I thank all the translators, actors and friends who advised, tweaked and glossed this translation. The original (English) text could not have been written without the help and support of its script editor, my wife, Georgina Van Welie. Finally, a word to thank all those collaborators, friends and colleagues who stayed up into the farthest reaches of the night during the various creations of this piece and who helped to make it what it eventually became.

Sulayman Al-Bassam
Writer-Director
Kuwait, February 2006

Production history

The Al-Hamlet Summit (English)

The English language production of the play was premiered on 7 August 2002 at the Pleasance Studios, Edinburgh, with the following cast:

Hamlet	Neil Edmond
Claudius	Nigel Barrett
Gertrude	Olivia Williams
Polonius/Fortinbras	Simon Kane
Ophelia/UN Messenger	Tea Alagic
Laertes	Ken Collard
Arms Dealer	Marlene Kaminsky

Written and Directed by	Sulayman Al-Bassam

Script Editor	Georgina Van Welie
Assistant Director	Nigel Barrett
Musical Director, Composer and Performer	Lewis Gibson
Music Composer and Performer	Alfredo Genovesi
Lighting Designer and Technical Manager	Richard Williamson

Co-Produced by
The Foreign Media Department, Ministry of Information, Kuwait

Touring history
Edinburgh International Fringe Festival (Fringe First Award Winner), UK 2002
Cairo International Festival of Experimental Theatre (Winner of Best Director; Best Production Awards), Egypt 2002

The Al-Hamlet Summit (Arabic)

The Arabic language production of the play was premiered on
14 February 2004. The production was co-produced by and presented
at the Tokyo International Arts Festival, Japan, with the following
cast:

Hamlet	Kefah Al-Khous
Claudius	Nicolas Daniel
Gertrude	Amana Wali
Polonius/Fortinbras	Monadhil Al-Bayati
Ophelia/UN Messenger	Mariam Ali
Laertes	Beshar Al-Ibrahim
Arms Dealer	Nigel Barrett

Written and Directed by	Sulayman Al-Bassam

Assistant Director	Nigel Barrett
Musical Director, Composer and Performer	Lewis Gibson
Music Composer and Performer	Alfredo Genovesi
Lighting Designer and Technical Manager	Richard Williamson
Production Manager	Mohamed Jawad Ahmad

Co-Produced by
The Tokyo International Arts Festival, Japan

Touring history
Tokyo International Arts Festival, Japan 2004
The Bath Shakespeare Festival, UK 2004
The Riverside Studios, London, UK 2004
Spotkania Festival, Warsaw, Poland 2004
Seoul Performing Arts Festival, South Korea 2004
Fajr Festival, Tehran, Iran 2005
Singapore International Arts Festival, Singapore 2005
Hamlet Summer Festival, Elsinore Castle, Denmark 2005
Winner of the Kuwait National Arts Award (Best Director), Kuwait
2004

The Al-Hamlet Summit

Delegates:
Claudius – The Ruler
Gertrude – His Wife
Hamlet – Her Son
Polonius – The Minister
Ophelia – His Daughter
Laertes – His Son

Outsiders:
Arms Dealer
Fortinbras

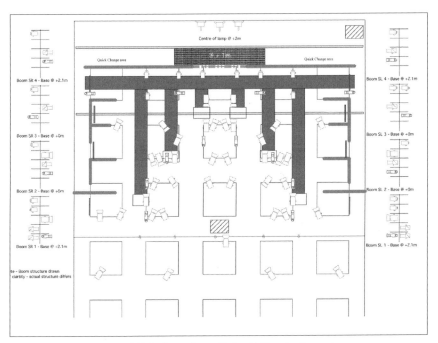

Stage and lighting plan of *The Al-Hamlet Summit*, 2004,
courtesy of Richard Williamson

Act One: Al-Fajr – Dawn[I]

⊹⊹⊹

A conference hall containing six conference desks.
Downstage centre, a roughly constructed grave.

A BURIAL:

The six delegates enter, each carrying a piece of the former leader's body wrapped in cloth. They place the dismembered body parts in the grave. Each delegate improvises a speech to the body part as it is laid in the grave.

Claudius exits as soon as he can. The others exit in turn.

1:

Enter Hamlet, then Gertrude.
Pre-session dialogue: through mics, hushed, urgent.

Gertrude: Why is your face so black, Hamlet?

Hamlet: It must be syphilis; I've been with one too many whores, Mama.

Gertrude: Is this wit?

Hamlet: Fact! There are many more whores than in my father's time.

Enter Laertes and Ophelia.

Gertrude: Hamlet!

Hamlet: You should take a stroll outside, look at the tall buildings, lit with neon; brothels, brothels!

Laertes: Welcome back, Prince. My condolences; may Allah increase your wages in heaven.

Hamlet: And yours in brothels, Laertes.

Laertes: My Lord?

Hamlet: No, no... I hold you in the highest esteem, Laertes; your father was a loyal, devoted, loving subject to mine, and I rely most entirely on your devotion to our line –

Enter Polonius.

Polonius: His Dread and most Honourable Majesty, All Mighty Leader of the Armed Forces, Commander of Air, Land and Sea; President Elect of this Noble Assembly begs your gracious attentions – session has begun.

Enter Claudius, all stand as the National Anthem bellows across the conference hall.

A bell announces the beginning of the session.

Claudius: In the Name of Allah, The Bounteous, The Merciful. *(The sound of the conference bell indicates the beginning of the session: all sit.)* By my decree 10,000 palms have been planted and 2 public gardens opened in my brother's memory. *(All clap.)* The time for mourning is over. Today the dawn bursts forth fertility and – like the phoenix that comes shimmering up in flames from its cold bed of dust – my wife from my brother's ashen hand has leapt, her cheek all moist with tears and wet with the dew of renewal, to partner me in this crowning enterprise: the dawn has risen upon the people of our nation: the New Democracy begins today! *(Assembly claps.)* The nation claps: I clap for the nation. We ride on the crest of a great wave, born of the will of the people and the needs of History: I am not its leader: I am its lamb. *(Clapping.)* Hamlet, you do not clap? Hamlet?

Hamlet: It is the heat, my Lord; it brings the worms up out of the earth and just beneath the film of our perfumes –

Claudius: No one doubts the enormity of your grief, Hamlet.

Hamlet: I am dazed by the stench of rot!

Claudius: You are morbid, when the world celebrates around you, you grieve while others rejoice, this fetish-sadness sits like a stain on the New Democracy: what is past is past, what is dead is dead, what rots will rot.

Hamlet: I'll spare you my afflictions, my studies await me; my flight leaves tonight.

Claudius: The invisible forces of evil besiege us from all sides: enemy leaflets circulate like rats in our midst; Fortinbras's troops armed with millions of dollars of foreign equipment are lined upon our border, if the city were quiet enough you could hear them breathe; you will not leave.

Hamlet rises from his desk.

Gertrude: Hamlet, I am your mother. The University has long been the source of regressive trends amongst us; already it has changed you: your father and I have deemed it council to keep you away from such throbbing beds of lunacy.

Hamlet: Closer to your throbbing beds of shame.

Gertrude: The country weeps with you, Hamlet, its wounds are open, and need your balming presence. Do not tar your father's memory with such eager departure. Do not force knives into your mother's bleeding heart. Stay with us, Hamlet.

Polonius: I will count.

They vote.

Hamlet: When I got off the plane I smelt her; on the runway, in his welcoming embrace in the guards' salute I smelt her. On his hand and on his cheek – her scent – on his neck and on his back and on his balls her scent. Oh God, I can smell her now. Oh filth, filth, he enters her, he goes inside, he does, he goes inside her again and again… I'll stay! *(Hamlet votes.)* I'll stay!

Claudius: Glorious solidarity blesses our nation's first assembly. Let enemies beware of the Nation United, let Fortinbras skulk upon our borders, I declare three days National Holiday in celebration of our New Democracy.

Polonius: Come, secretaries and ministers: the press, the people, the world awaits.

A bell announces the end of the session.

Exit all except Hamlet and Ophelia.

2:

Hamlet, Ophelia. Prayers in the distance from many sides.

Hamlet: Why are you spying on me?

Ophelia: I'm looking at you.

Hamlet: And I… am looking at you.

Ophelia: I will go, then.

Hamlet: No, no – Ophelia?

Ophelia: I'm here.

Hamlet: Has it been so long?

Ophelia: 3 summers... I got your tapes, thank you.

Hamlet: My tapes...

Ophelia: I know them all by heart. "When the skies fall in and the seas are set ablaze..."

Hamlet: It was a different world then.

Ophelia: And me?

Hamlet: You're a woman now.

Ophelia: Won't you look at me?

Hamlet: Now?

Ophelia: Why not?

Hamlet: Not now – I will, I will – I long to look at you, to stare at you, to drink from the sight of you, but not now. I can't. Perhaps it's the heat, my blood is not used to this heat, my blood is not what it used to be – I do love you, in my heart of hearts and with my own body I love you. Go now... (*Writing.*) Through the interminable night that awaits us... With your own eyes.

Jets pass in the distance overhead.

3:

Enter Polonius, Claudius.

Polonius: I've got 300 men working round the clock gathering up the leaflets.

Claudius: Forget the leaflets, burn the townships, all of them – I want them all burnt by dawn.

Enter Gertrude.

Gertrude: What's the schedule for tomorrow?

Polonius: Breakfast with the Russians first thing, press conference, then it's the opening of the New Parliament. Madame will be with us?

Gertrude: Yes.

Ophelia returns to her desk.

A bell announces the beginning of the session.

Claudius: *(At his desk.)* What remains for today, Polonius?

Polonius: My son, my Lord, asks your permission to leave the city.

Claudius: Why?

Laertes: To join the ranks of the valiant defenders of our nation's sovereignty.

Claudius: Good, a young man like him needs to see some action. Let him be stationed in the South, in front of Fortinbras and overseeing the militias.

Laertes: I will do all in my power to be worthy of this honour.

Claudius: I'll make him a general.

Polonius: My Lord!

Claudius: Nothing is too much for the son of Polonius.

Polonius: I am forever yours.

Claudius: I thank you all for your devotion. Time is neither with us nor against us, our enemies are vigilant, they scurry while we sleep. I bid you all good night.

A bell announces the end of the session.

Exit Hamlet, Laertes, Ophelia.

Gertrude: I have a proposal. It concerns Ophelia.

Polonius: What has she done?

Gertrude: Laertes is leaving. She will be so alone.

Polonius: She has many pursuits; she is an excellent pianist, reads profusely, rides regularly, speaks French, German and Czech.

Claudius: She is very beautiful.

Gertrude: Hamlet, given that he's staying with us, is likely to have far

too much time on his hands: Ophelia is vulnerable.

Polonius: Do you suspect my daughter of anything?

Gertrude: I am a woman, Polonius, and I sense the seeds of scandal before they are blasted on to the wind. I am also a mother and a wife. My son has long been of an inclination towards your French-speaking, piano-riding, horse-playing daughter and now he is of an age. I propose their marriage. Claudius?

Claudius: What has this to do with the New Democracy?

Polonius: It would be one of its symbols.

Claudius: It would entertain the press?

Polonius: A sense of shared responsibility, my Lord, may help the Prince overcome this negativity towards the New Order.

Claudius: Marriage would geld him.

Polonius: Madame, our house is no stranger to royalty; honour and blood have tied us together over centuries; my daughter will be delighted.

They vote. Motion carried.

Gertrude: Excellent.

Polonius: Marvellous.

Claudius: The future is ever brightening. To the New Democracy!

Polonius and Gertrude: The New Democracy!

A bell announces the end of the session.

Exit Gertrude.

Claudius: The townships, Polonius.

Polonius: I'll give orders to start the burning immediately.

They exit.

4:

Enter Laertes, clearing his desk. Enter Ophelia.

Ophelia: To the mountains?

Laertes: Yes.

Ophelia: You'll die, Laertes, they'll send me a photo of you hanging from a tree.

Laertes: I cannot do diplomacy; we sit and talk like drunkards, waiting for others to solve our problems.

Ophelia: Wait just a few days, things will settle.

Laertes: Nothing will settle Fortinbras but a bullet in his head. Look at me: I'll miss you. Your eyes, Ophelia, your eyes... They are not the innocent jades they used to be, another colour has tinged them. A little sparkle, or, or, or a little breeze, or, or, or a little... aching? An aching in your eyes, Ophelia, the aching of virgin fields for the plough? When the world lies frightened in its bed do you pour lotions over your body and move in time with the breeze? I know you do, but that is not what courts and Kings are for, is it? What are they for? Capturing, invading, sacking, splitting: virgin thighs, virgin honour, virgin sex; your name, spiked on the royal cock, our titles spattered with royal cum, and poor sister of Laertes left heaped on the floor among the broken shells of promises and the burnt-out shitloads of gold. Never, Ophelia, never! Tame this lust in your eyes, tame it, woman, before I tame it for you.

Enter Polonius.

Polonius: General Laertes!

Laertes salutes his father and exits.

Ophelia: Don't leave me.

Polonius: They tell me you have been lurking in orchards with the Prince Hamlet as the sun goes down. Or was it by the pool? Where do you lurk exactly?

Ophelia: We walk sometimes at dusk before the evening prayers.

Polonius: Don't walk at dusk, don't walk at night, don't walk at dawn and don't walk at noon. Right now I want to be able to hear your footsteps at all times, wherever you walk will be within the orbit of my hearing, within the circle of my infinite love; right now my love describes the boundaries of your universe; don't walk outside it into the abyss beyond, where your footsteps and your cries will go unheard. What's the time?

Ophelia: Near midnight.

Polonius: Get to bed, there may be trouble tonight.

Polonius returns to his desk.

Gertrude enters Claudius's office, they begin making love.

5:

Hamlet, praying at his father's grave.

Hamlet: Let the skies fall in and the seas be set ablaze, let the material world collapse and markets go untended; let wild beasts roam through cities and infant girls be buried alive for no crime; make Hell fires burn fiercely and bring Paradise near; but lay the records upon, inspire me with your command, show me my labours, I hold my life in no esteem, I carry not an atom's weight of good, I have grown fat with idle life, let me not be mad, but lay the records upon, inspire me with your command, inspire me with your command – *(the love-making in the conference room climaxes)* who's there? Who is it?

Arms Dealer: A friend.

Hamlet: What do you want?

Arms Dealer: No, please I understand you perfectly in Arabic. Sorry I'm –

Hamlet: I know who you are.

Arms Dealer: Not disturbing you, am I? I –

Hamlet: Stay.

Arms Dealer: Needed some air: couldn't breathe in the hotel.

Hamlet: It's the fires, they have started the fires.

Arms Dealer: Mmm. Your father was a great man; the world is not the same for his loss.

Hamlet: Are you American?

Arms Dealer: *(Quoting.)* "Vast oceans of savagery consume the world, false authority towers from Mecca to Jerusalem, from Jerusalem to the Americas and man is on the brink of a great precipice..."[2]

Hamlet: How do you know that? Those are his words.

Arms Dealer hands him a green leaflet.

Hamlet: I can't see, give me a light.

He holds out a lighter.

Hamlet: (*Reading.*) "Forensic evidence leaked from the post mortem indicates that our great leader was murdered. His cardiac arrest was induced by sodium nitrate injected into his ear via a syringe, an assassination technique commonly used by the secret police under the leadership of his brother and assassin Claudius." Where did you find this?

Arms Dealer: They're all over.

Hamlet: (*Reading on.*) "Whilst Hamlet, the late King's son, continues to lead the life of the Murtad dissolute, gambling and whoring the nation's millions in the playgrounds of Europe." Oh God! "The People's – The People's" – bring the light closer – "Liberation Brigade will avenge this sickening murder and will show no mercy to those who weep and mourn, weep and gnash their teeth (*the Arms Dealer lights the leaflet*)... the evil forces of imperialism have found a willing agent in the figure of Claudius..."

Arms Dealer withdraws.

Jets pass screaming overhead, as hundreds of leaflets fall from the sky.

Hamlet: "Raise your might and God's holy wrath against the horned Satan that soils our earth and the Greater Satan that enslaves our people and the world. We will not rest until God's labours are done. We will not rest until His labours are done."

Hamlet gathers some leaflets and exits.

6:

Hamlet: *(Shaking.)* My father's murdered – *(Trying to speak, but unable.)*

Ophelia holds him for a long time, he weeps.

Ophelia: I'm here – I'm here –

Hamlet: Be with me –

Ophelia: Always.

Hamlet: Hold me.

Ophelia: I love you – I love you.

Black out.

END OF ACT ONE

Act Two: Al-Zuhr – Noon

✠

1:

Morning.

Ophelia, alone at her desk, wearing a headscarf.

Polonius: *(At his desk.)* Today is a very good-looking day, correct? A day for positive images, rousing words, transparent communication, and I need you to look the part, Ophelia – what the hell is that? Are you mad? *(Walks briskly over to her and snatches her headscarf.)* What's this?

Ophelia: I'm more comfortable like this.

Polonius: You look like a terrorist! Do you know how many photographers are out there? Why are you crying?

Ophelia: Last night –

Polonius: Last night what?

Ophelia: Hamlet...

Polonius: Hamlet!

Ophelia: ...needed some help with his speech, but the speech was not making sense; shells fell all night, the fires burnt all night and the electricity cut out around three. It was a bad night. That is all.

Hamlet enters, goes to Claudius's desk, takes out files and begins skimming through memos.

Polonius: *(Finding green leaflets of PLB.)* Where did you get these?

Ophelia: I don't know.

Polonius: Answer me!

Ophelia: He brought them.

Polonius: This runs deep, Ophelia, very deep. I only hope I can save you from the fallout. Come with me. Come, come, come. *(Senses someone rummaging at Claudius's desk.)* Hamlet? *(Hamlet runs away.)* Hamlet!

2:

Enter Arms Dealer, Claudius.

Arms Dealer: Your Highness!!... Power suits you. You look like a King.

Claudius: I was not expecting you so soon.

Arms Dealer: Early bird catches the worm.

Claudius: And blood draws flies.

Arms Dealer: Buzz, buzz, Claude.

Claudius: Keep your voice down.

Arms Dealer: This is a most echoey corridor, you should have it filled, busts, statues, fallen enemies, stuffed and garroted, I know some excellent sculptors.

Claudius: How long will you be staying with us?

Arms Dealer: As long as I am welcome.

Claudius: We are preparing for war. It may not be in your interest to stay here very long.

Arms Dealer: I'm on a little tour. He called me yesterday, most upset I have not been to visit him yet, you know how emotional he gets – "You filthy double-crosser, you promised me this, that – be careful, you're not dealing with the Chechnyans now!" – *(Laughs.)*

Claudius: Who's this?

Arms Dealer: Fortinbras!

Claudius: *Inshallah*, everything's okay?

Arms Dealer: He's so endearing, so forward looking, so modern somehow.

Claudius: I'll send you a crate of – what is it you like – Bordeaux? I am so happy you are with us.

Arms Dealer: So am I.

Claudius: We'll have a party.

Arms Dealer: No!

Claudius: Yes, a large one. I want you to meet the ministers.

Arms Dealer: I'd love to meet them, of course.

Claudius: Tomorrow – this evening! I'll arrange it. You must excuse me. The New Parliament's opening in (*looks at watch*) –

Arms Dealer: 2 hours and 12 minutes – I know. Good luck.

3:

Bell announces the beginning of the session.

Polonius: A minister's loyalty to his King and country goes beyond the rational bonds of duty. A love that defies the usual spheres of human employment. A love, that in my case, can be compared to the loyalty of the last soldier, that unsung hero, who, knee-deep in comrades' blood, surrounded by thousands of enemy tanks, helicopters, infantry and mortar, swells with the knowledge of imminent death, bulges with patriotism, fires the last rounds from his outdated Russian rifle and falls, struck by a bullet to the heart that continues to beat for at least 2 hours more! Irrational love! Absolute devotion! Complete surrender to the will of King and country – THAT is what I offer.

Gertrude: Does my breakfast have to suffer this man's devotion?

Polonius: My breakfasts are yours, Madame.

Claudius: Explain yourself.

Polonius: (*Adjusts his position.*) If I were able to explain this matter to myself, I would be much better placed to explain myself; but this matter is far beyond... Your son is mad, Madame! Mad! He is being drawn further and further into extremist circles of thought and action and he is mad I tell you!

Claudius: The Parliament opens in less than an hour.

Polonius: A matter of minutes: Ophelia.

Ophelia stands up and reads Hamlet's poems.

Ophelia: The refugee who stands at the wire fence of your heart –
         no numbers to his name, no credit, no guns;
         all sewage and exile,
         lays siege to your soul, with the pain of his songs.

Polonius: Note the paranoiac tendency in this innocent-seeming foul-smelling ditty. Note the distrust of all authority.

Ophelia: When the worlds fall apart
         And the skies cave in

Enter Hamlet.

When Hell fires consume the light
And Paradise is brought nearer this earth:
On that day, know that I am looking for you.

Exit Hamlet.

Polonius: Note the apocalyptic imagery. Note the yearning for violent and comprehensive change to the world order. I have studies that will elucidate further on the links between this sort of fantasy and terrorist activities.

Gertrude: These poems are the work of an adolescent, Polonius, they prove nothing!

Polonius: Now, look at what I found in his drawers! *(Displays PLB leaflets.)* Not one, not ten, but thousands of them, thousands!

Claudius: This is capital!

Ophelia: Grief can force –

Gertrude: Grief, yes! Grief!

Ophelia: Temporary insanity!

Claudius: The marriage must be delayed.

Ophelia: What marriage?

Gertrude: Until we have more proof of how far his grief may have

changed him.

Claudius: More proof then, Polonius?

Ophelia: What marriage?

Polonius: My daughter will supply proof.

Ophelia: What marriage!!

Gertrude: Really? How?

Polonius: Ophelia?

Ophelia: Yes?

Polonius: The next time you meet with Hamlet you will ask him – in a roundabout and honeyed way – questions like, "Where have you been? What have you been writing? What are you doing with your nights?"

Ophelia: You think I can do that?

Gertrude: You'll make an excellent liar.

Ophelia: I lack your Highness's skill.

Gertrude: Sorry, what did she say?

Claudius: We were all born bad liars, you'll learn. Ask him – "Do you go to the mosques?"

Polonius: "Who are your friends? What are they called?"

Claudius: "What are you reading?"

Gertrude: Someone should be with her, she could lie.

Polonius: We'll be with her, Madame; leave it to me: *(Proposing a motion.)* "The Royal Marriage to be delayed, pending further proof of the Prince's seditious leanings."

They vote: motion is carried.

Exit Ophelia.

Claudius: "They deceive and God deceives, but God is the greatest of Deceivers!"

Bell announces the end of the session.

Exit all.

4:

Hamlet, alone in the desert, in the distance we hear the sound of a military band and pronouncements on the occasion of the opening of the New Parliament.

Hamlet: The villages of my heart have been emptied,
their pavements orphaned to the wind.
All spirit of man in me aged between 14 and 60
Has been taken down to the waterfront
And settled head-first in the shallows.
When noon walks across the square like a widow,
I am the ghost bell that swings on churches
I am the minaret with its tongue in the sand
I am the child with a bullet in its arm weeping amongst
the rocks;
I am the mute that contemplates the ape
while the wind writes my shame upon the sea.

Enter Arms Dealer.

Arms Dealer: You're not at the opening.

Hamlet: Celebration's lost its charms.

Arms Dealer: We're alike, we prefer being in the shadows.

Hamlet: Are you following me?

Arms Dealer: Maybe.

Hamlet: How's the hotel?

Arms Dealer: Been upgraded. There's a lot of talk about you: some people think you're still in Europe, others say you're planning to escape, but nobody really knows what you're doing, do they?

Hamlet: (*Looking at the horizon.*) When I was young the horizon had more colours, more light, more promise...

Arms Dealer: I was thinking, perhaps, we could be friends. You need someone to confide in and I know what it is like to be isolated. You have a great future, we would like to develop something with you, promote your agenda.

Hamlet: What do you know about phosphorus?

Arms Dealer: It makes little white puffs of smoke, like a barbecue.

Hamlet: Does it burn?

Arms Dealer: Haven't you heard the story of the gravedigger's baby?

Hamlet: Tell me.

Arms Dealer: When the curfew was over, the baby was 5 days dead, and they brought it to the gravedigger. He prepared a deep and narrow grave, and when the prayers were done, he shovelled the first mound of earth into it: the tiny corpse exploded into flames and the gravedigger was blinded. That's phosphorus.

Hamlet: Can you sell me some?

Arms Dealer: I can.

Hamlet: Good.

Arms Dealer: It is necessary for a Prince to understand how to avail himself of the beast and the man. If men were entirely good this would not hold, but because –

An explosion in the distance, the military band has gone silent and is replaced by sirens.

Hamlet: What was that?

Arms Dealer: I've no idea.

They exit together.

5:

Enter Claudius, Polonius.

Claudius: Find them!

Polonius: No one has claimed responsibility, no tip-offs, no calls, nothing.

Claudius: The pipeline is on the rocks –

Polonius: I have got 20 PLB members under torture –

Claudius: The investors are terrified!

Polonius: The Shia leaders are being rounded up, I've got 50 mobile squadrons in a net around the city, men scouring the sewers, whoever they are, they will not escape me.

Claudius: I want the car-bombers' faces across the papers by tomorrow. Or I'll write your resignation for you.

Enter Laertes.

Polonius: I have summoned you, Laertes, to brief us on developments in the South.

Claudius: What news with you, Laertes?

Laertes: My Lord, the signs of war are gathering fast. Until this morning, Fortinbras had 3,000 men stationed 20 miles south of our border. Apart from two small skirmishes, all has been quiet for the last two days. But one hour before dawn a convoy appeared on the horizon that threw fear into the souls of our men and had civilian families running in droves for their cars. Over the hills came not a convoy, but a juggernaut, a 15 mile column of Merkava and British Centurion tanks – three tanks abreast – moving at 15 mph towards our border. It was as if Fortinbras's entire army was advancing upon us as one giant armoured centipede. The Merkavas and the Centurions tore up the tarmac surface of the highway as they advanced and bathed the landscape in a blue fog of exhaust smoke. They have moved up so much equipment that the coastal highway and the sea are covered with tanks and heavy artillery for 20 miles.3

Claudius: We are familiar with these tactics, Laertes; I see no cause for alarm.

Hamlet enters carrying a piece of an exploded vehicle, affecting deafness from the explosion.

Polonius: Where were you?

Hamlet: Sorry I'm late. Have you seen the traffic?

Laertes: *(To Claudius.)* No cause for alarm, my Lord?

Polonius: You weren't at the Parliament?

Hamlet: What?

Polonius: Parliament!

Claudius: *(To Laertes.)* None.

Hamlet: Lament? Lament!?

Polonius: Where were you?

Hamlet: I'm finished with laments. Tell Uncle. Finished. There's a party out there! Hundreds, thousands, all spattered in blood, screaming in the streets! Ecstatic masses foaming with nationalistic ecstasy. It's brilliant!

Claudius: Hamlet, there was a terrorist attack at the opening.

Hamlet: Here we are. Look, oh look!

Claudius: A terrorist attack.

Hamlet: Quack? What Quack? Quack Quack! I found this!

Polonius: He's mad!

Hamlet: It's a trophy. I'm giving it to Ophelia as a sign of my bleeding heart! No, too sad. I'm giving it to Uncle! Yes! Uncle! Give me a kiss and I'll give you this trophy.

Claudius: We'll leave him.

Hamlet: Oh come, Uncle, your kisses aren't as prized as Ophelia's lips. Please take it, Uncle, give it to Mother as a sign of your mis-shaped love, oh she'll love it. Uncle, the nation's will is in my arms, take it from me –

Polonius: My Lord, we're leaving you now.

Hamlet: Uncle! Uncle!

Black out.

END OF ACT TWO

Act Three: Al-Asr – Mid-Afternoon

✛

1.1:

TIME: 7:45

Arms Dealer: Parliament opened with a bang!

Polonius: Listen to this. *(Opens a folder and reads.)* "The treacherous enemy are dwarves. They spit at the giant, but the giant picks them up and crushes them. They are traitors, pirates and mercenaries."

Arms Dealer: We call them terrorists.

Polonius: I like this word. Will you write it for me? *(Offering him a pen.)*

Arms Dealer: Of course. *(Writing.)*

Polonius: Terro-ri!

Arms Dealer: Terro-rist.

Polonius: Terror-roo!

Arms Dealer: Terror-rist.

Polonius: Terror – um!

Arms Dealer: Terrorist!

Polonius: Terrorist! Excellent word, much money in this word.

Arms Dealer: Yes... About the money.

Polonius: Money? No problem, no problem, *habibi.*

Arms Dealer: When?

Polonius: When? When? What does it mean when?

Arms Dealer: Upon signing of the contract.

Polonius: In full?

Arms Dealer: In full. (*Arms Dealer pockets Polonius's pen and exits.*)

Polonius: My pen... Terrorist!

1.2:

TIME: 10:15

Hamlet: Who is Claudius?

Laertes: You don't get it, do you?

Hamlet: Who is he?

Laertes: Our supreme and sovereign leader.

Hamlet: Take my eyes, my nose, my sword, my women! Are you a tribesman, Laertes?

Laertes: What do you want? The labourer has no factory to work in and the thinkers are all asthmatic and wheezing?

Hamlet: "As you are, in such a way you will be ruled."

Laertes: The people need a God!

Hamlet: Fine. I know where you stand.

Laertes: Forcing internal division is political suicide: the strategy of an angry child.

Hamlet: He is a murderer.

Laertes: So are all leaders.

Hamlet: He killed my father.

Laertes: Fortinbras wrote that line, it's enemy propaganda and you know it.

Hamlet: I'll prove it!

Laertes: Well, let me know.

Hamlet: I want you with me here, Laertes, the real fight is here.

Laertes: And let me know when you've finished.

Hamlet: What?

Laertes: Apologising for your own futility.

1.3:

TIME: 13:30

Gertrude: Where was that – Paris?

Arms Dealer: Zurich.

Gertrude: Of course! Zurich! And how are your dogs?

Arms Dealer: I've just acquired a magnificent Pekinese stud.

Gertrude: And I have my Mexican Hairless bitch – we must introduce them!

Arms Dealer: What a monster we will make.

Gertrude: You are such a charmer.

Arms Dealer: You are such a purebred!

Gertrude: Is there anything I can get you?

Arms Dealer: You are so kind. Anything I can get you?

Gertrude: You're so cavalier! I don't want to trouble you, but I have a farm in the South – my private retreat: it needs some work, it doesn't feel safe anymore and I was wondering if you might –

Arms Dealer: I just love the countryside! I believe I'm already familiar with the place.

Gertrude: Really?

Arms Dealer: *(Showing her some photos.)* This it? You look so magnificent in your natural state!

Gertrude: I'll keep these if you don't mind.

Arms Dealer: They're only copies, I'm afraid.

Gertrude: As I said, it needs tighter security.

Arms Dealer: My pleasure. Where are we going?

Gertrude: To the sea, you don't mind, do you?

Arms Dealer: I smell it from here.

1.4:

TIME: 13:32

Hamlet: The enemy on the border is the illusion they feed you, the illusion they want you to believe.

Laertes: People are dying everyday, I see them, I see the bombs that kill them, I see the soldiers that fire them, I hear the politicians that direct them, it's not an illusion.

Hamlet: The real enemy is here, in the palace, amongst us.

Laertes: There will be no nation to fight over unless we defeat Fortinbras.

Hamlet: We'll have no nation to lose unless we destroy the rot that devours it from within.

Laertes: Hamlet, may God go with you. I'm leaving you this. *(Places a pistol on the table.)*

Exit Laertes.

Hamlet: Laertes! My brother.

2:

Gertrude is with Ophelia, she presents her with jewelry: a necklace, a bracelet, a ring – the taqam that is traditionally presented to Arab brides.

Ophelia: Who are these from?

Gertrude: From Hamlet! Now look, no politics, no religion: talk about love, not sex, love. He's so *fleur a peau*, he cannot bear *vulgarity* – ask him about his poems, request some more, nothing silly or girlish please, you know how intelligent he is, you must keep him interested!

Ophelia: A –

Gertrude: And don't cry! When you are married, you will look back at all this and laugh out loud.

Ophelia: We will, we'll laugh.

Hamlet: (*At his desk, holding the pistol Laertes left him.*)
It doesn't weigh much, why should it?
It delivers. It has a number on it. It's well made;
Its coil, mechanism, bolt and trigger have
Evolved over centuries, its secrets embezzled
From father to son, it is a perfect machine.
It is mine to polish with Egyptian cottons
while I career dreamsick, from office to office,
slowly murdering the fire that made my soul,
feeding my disease from door to door,
round and round this porn shop of sores.
No martyr's passion blazing in this body,
No vision of heaven,
no yearning for justice, no aching for change,
my intestine is like a pig's:
It baulks at nothing;
my hatred as imperfect as my love;
nothing heroic, nothing repulsive,
just a futile mediocrity, made bearable by my disease,
that drowns with a torturer's patience and criminal ease
the fires that made my soul
from here to the day I die.
(*Reading the serial number on the pistol.*) 552497.
The disease I carry is stronger than me,

This disease I call Myself.
The self is a bitch that won't let go.

Enter Claudius and Polonius, wearing long black abats and burkhas.

Claudius: Thank you, Gertrude.

Gertrude adjusts the black abats that cover the two men from head to toe.
She exits.

Polonius and Claudius prompt Ophelia in the opening lines of this dialogue.

Ophelia: Hamlet, I am praying for you.

Claudius taps her on the back to speak louder.

Ophelia: Hamlet, I am praying for you.

Hamlet: Ophelia! I can hear your prayers.

Ophelia: Thank you for your gifts.

Hamlet: What gifts?

Ophelia: It doesn't matter.

Hamlet: I don't know if I have ever told you...

Ophelia: Don't...

Hamlet: I must, I have this terrible need to change myself, or rather, rather there is a change that is coming...

Ophelia: Don't tell me now –

Hamlet: And if I don't tell you now...

Ophelia: Tell me now then, tell me, speak!

Hamlet: Ophelia?

Ophelia: Yes.

Hamlet: What gifts? What gifts! (*Long pause.*) Has it come?

Ophelia: What?

Hamlet: The hour that takes you away from me?

Ophelia: No!

Hamlet: Must I be forced to hate you now?

Ophelia: No! It is far away, very far.

Hamlet: But the hour has come.

Ophelia: I am still here.

Hamlet: No, no you are gone.

Ophelia: You love me.

Hamlet: No, no. I do not blame you, but, but, but...

Ophelia: Try to love me...

Hamlet: Nor can I forgive you, you do understand?

Ophelia: Don't do this.

Hamlet: How can I love you!?

Ophelia: Try...

Claudius and Polonius smother her mouth.

Hamlet: I will clean this land, I will make it pure, I understand, I do understand, but I will cleanse it for you, I will prepare it for your return, even if it costs me my life, I will clean it, I will purge it, blood will flow, I will make blood flow in torrents, I swear in my father's name, I swear in the name of Allah but you will return, Ophelia, you will return. *(Exits.)*

Ophelia: *(Sung.)*

> My master, where are you going?
> Ai! Why don't you take me with you?
> Take me to the town.
> Ai! To sell me to the *bazargi*
> For a pinch of gold
> To gild the palace door.4

Exit Ophelia.

A bell announces the beginning of the session.

Gertrude: She is ruining my son's mind. I want her sent to the farms.

Polonius: What farms, Madame?

Gertrude: The work farms in the South. She can work on mine. She is to go.

Polonius: Madame is enraged. This ugliness offends her and blurs her judgement –

Claudius: Gertrude, we refuse haste.

Gertrude: I insist.

Claudius: Polonius, let her seek refuge outside the city for a few days. Marriage will not be spoken of again. It puts our son in ill humour. Investments are, however, crucial to the economy at this stage of the war-effort, there are car bombs exploding at every corner, we have not seen a tourist in weeks and his temperament seems regressive and unconducive to the common good, national security demands that Hamlet too is sent away. Where to, Madame?

Gertrude: Beirut?

Polonius: Too many militias.

Gertrude: Damascus?

Claudius: Too many thinkers.

Polonius: Cairo?

Gertrude: Too many liars. Sana'a?

Polonius: Too many rebels.

Claudius: Rabat?

Gertrude: Too many druggies.

Claudius: Khartoum?

Polonius: Too many blacks.

Gertrude: Jeddah?

Claudius: Too many sticks.

Gertrude: Tehran?

Claudius: Too many turbans.

Polonius: Paris?

Claudius: Too many women.

Gertrude: Washington?

Polonius: He'd never get in.

Claudius: London?

Polonius and Gertrude: London!![5]

Claudius: Get him on the next plane to London, call the foreign secretary, tell him he's coming to gamble along Piccadilly, book him 3 months at Claridges and give him a state cheque book.

Polonius: My Lord, Fortinbras's tanks shelled the airport this morning, the tarmac is in ribbons.

Claudius: Close the highway, he can use that to take off.

Polonius: I'll count.

They vote.

Polonius: Carried.

Gertrude: My son cannot leave without a proper send-off!

Polonius: She's right, it might reflect badly.

Claudius: A party then!

Polonius: A small state occasion.

Jets pass overhead.

Bomb blasts in the distance.

Claudius: The future is bright. I thank you.

A bell indicates the end of the session.

Delegates rise to leave, but as Claudius lingers in the corridor –

Enter Hamlet.

Hamlet: Hell's plagues on your mother and your mother's mother and your mother's mother's mother. Do not gawp at me, you imperialist dog! Don't stare at me, you leader-by-proxy! Agent! Do you know whose son I am! His name makes you tremble!!

Exit Claudius.

Hamlet: Futile man! *(To the musicians.)* Hey you. I need you to cleanse my soul, play for me. Play an old, old *Maqa'am*.

They play.

3:

Ophelia: Are you the devil?

Arms Dealer: Are you attracted to me, young lady?

Ophelia: If I am?

Arms Dealer: Have you ever been with a man before? Alone in the dark?

Ophelia: *(Silence.)*

Arms Dealer: You are trembling, come closer.

Ophelia: Lean your face towards me, close your eyes.

She pulls out a knife.

Arms Dealer: You're so passionate *(twisting her arm and throwing her to the floor, she cries in pain)*, oh the sweet yelp of pain – oh angels of the night, hide your virgin faces; the devil has one of your flock in his grasp! Drop the knife. What do you want, Ophelia, I satisfy all desires, what is it you want?

Ophelia: I want a bomb. *Qumbila*.

Arms Dealer: *Qubla?* A kiss? A kiss! Say it again!

Ophelia: Give me a kiss!

Arms Dealer: A bomb!

Ophelia: A bomb!

Arms Dealer: Kiss!

Ophelia: Kiss!

Arms Dealer: Bomb!

Ophelia: Bomb!

Arms Dealer: A little one or a big one?

Ophelia: Any.

4:

Hamlet, alone, contemplating a sacred area in the playing space.

Hamlet: This empty space. Why is it empty? This pit that our words fall into to die. This is where our secrets are buried, where our crimes gather – here in this space that nobody crosses. *(Standing on the edge of the empty space.)* At this point our feet tremble and we turn away our gazes from this Empty Quarter that... *(Enters the empty space.)* Here. This is where I shall dig and dance; unearth the foundations of this palace and summon up the little shreds of truth from this mass grave of lies. I'll have them up and out; I want them screamed across the corridors, streaking naked across the gardens, then who could say that Hamlet stood by and did nothing?

5:

Enter Polonius reading a map.

Gertrude: Here?

Polonius: Yes.

Gertrude: Are you sure, Polonius?

Polonius: He was most insistent, Madame, he even drew me a map!

Gertrude: Let me see.

Enter Claudius.

Claudius: You're joking!

Gertrude: Claudius, it's his last night.

Claudius: Find somewhere else.

Gertrude: Don't be ridiculous!

Claudius: I have never stood there, no one has ever stood there, I do not see why I should stand there to humour the whims of your sick child.

Gertrude: Claudius, please!

Claudius: Polonius, get out of there immediately!

Enter Arms Dealer.

Arms Dealer: Good evening, your majesties.

Gertrude: Hello! What a surprise.

Claudius enters the sacred space.

Claudius: We have been waiting for you.

Arms Dealer: Hamlet told me you were having a little occasion.

Claudius: I am so happy you could make it.

Arms Dealer: You look splendid, Madame.

Gertrude: Merci. *(Enter Ophelia.)* God, Ophelia, you look half-dead.

Polonius: She has been a little under the weather.

Ophelia: I have been throwing up all afternoon.

Arms Dealer: Poor child, do you have a fever?

Ophelia: Don't touch me!

Gertrude: She is upset that Hamlet is leaving.

Polonius: On the contrary, she is upset because she is leaving tomorrow.

Arms Dealer: I'm only trying to help.

Polonius: Thank you!

Claudius: Television been arranged?

Polonius: They're filming as we speak. Delayed transmission, of course.

Claudius: What's the order of events?

Polonius: We'll shake hands and embrace, swig some juice and before you know it he'll be on the plane.

Claudius: I'm sweating.

Polonius: I'm sorry. *(Polonius dabs Claudius's brow with a handkerchief.)*

Enter Hamlet on a papier-mâché horse. This scene is played by Hamlet with hysterical speed.

Hamlet: Good evening, tribe, family, friends.

Gertrude: Hamlet! What is this nonsense?

Hamlet: Nonsense! I am preparing for war, haven't you heard the enemy are on the borders! Ask him! Tonight we honour the elders! And stroke the horse! The horse of war!

Polonius: Why is your horse blinkered, my Lord?

Hamlet: To protect it from the glances of envy and Ophelia's poisoned smile.

Arms Dealer: Is the horse hungry, my Lord?

Hamlet: Ravenous, always! Horse of war!

Arms Dealer: A horse of war must munch, my Lord! *(Arms Dealer produces some sugar cubes.)*

Hamlet: Ah! Sugar cubes, what a noble warrior! Please feed the horse of war. Uncle, as with all things, you must start. Ummm...

Hamlet lunges at Claudius and stabs him with a stage knife. Claudius gasps. Hamlet withdraws the stage knife, pushes the blade in with his finger and laughs. His horse's head droops –

Oh, it's dying! Sodium nitrate, Uncle quickly! Oh, if Mother could weep, my horse might rise again, not a tear, Mother? Dried up? *(As Gertrude kneels to approach Hamlet, he gnaws her ear viciously.)*

Oh, look, it's rising, thank God Mother has some moistness left in her! Risen erect. Uncle could not kill it! Of course not, indigestion, that's all – *(Hamlet grabs Polonius by the testicles.)* Horse of WAR! Munch some more! Stroke it, Mother, but don't kiss it, it is a very randy horse.

Ophelia – you look pregnant – Uncle, have you sent her to the front yet? *(As Hamlet delivers these lines, the horse nuzzles Ophelia's breast and rubs its head against her groin.)* She really must make a visit – raise the morale of all those thousands! *(Ophelia exits. Hamlet to the Arms Dealer.)* Oh, but you, you are all sugar, it is enough for the horse to lick your hand. Now let us sing *(starting a tune)*: "Our blood is the price – oh cowards you are lice – but glory gory glory to the nation!" *(The others join in reluctantly.)*

To war! I thank you all. To war! To war!

Exit Hamlet.

Claudius: We are sending him to London, for tests.

Arms Dealer: I know some specialists.

Gertrude: Really? Perhaps you could give me their names.

Arms Dealer: Gladly.

Polonius: How would you like to present this affair to the nation, my Lord?

Claudius: As is!

Gertrude: What is that terrible noise?

Claudius: What's going on, Polonius?

Polonius: Some interference on the intercom, don't worry, my Lord.

Hamlet, over the conference loudspeakers.

Hamlet: Wait, please, wait, please.

Claudius: Sort this out!

Arms Dealer: Perhaps he's armed.

Claudius: Polonius, you dog!

Hamlet: There's more, my dears.

Claudius: This is unacceptable.

Over the speakers, Hamlet's voice repeating "Uncle, Uncle".

Gertrude: Hamlet, stop this immediately.

Claudius: Polonius – your gun!

Hamlet: Ladies and Gentlemen!

Hamlet reveals a large-scale cartoon of Gertrude lying on Old Hamlet's corpse, being penetrated by Claudius who is being penetrated by the Arms Dealer, all of whom have a knife wedged in the corpse. Hamlet fires blanks from a Kalashnikov into the air, trilling the sounds of a tribal wedding party.

Polonius: Guards! Guards! Guards!

6:

A bell announces the beginning of the session.

Claudius: He is a threat! I want him liquidated.

Gertrude: I'll speak to him.

Claudius: Polonius!

Polonius: My Lord!

Gertrude: I said I'll speak to him.

Claudius: Give the order.

Gertrude: My sex, Claudius! My sex tames your allies, my sex undermines your enemies, galvanises the masses and underwrites your loans. Nothing without me, do you realise? Nothing! I will speak to my son.

Claudius: By tomorrow.

Polonius: I'll accompany Madame. We must fear the worst.

Claudius: Thank you, my Wife. *(Exit Gertrude.)* I've emptied the funds, Polonius, you'll see me later about your needs.

Polonius: The generals are waiting for your directi–

Claudius: Let them wait!

Exit Polonius.

7:

Claudius: *(Alone, opening a briefcase full of dollars.)* Oh God: Petro dollars. Teach me the meaning of petro dollars.

I have no other God than you, I am created in your image, I seek guidance from you the All Seeing, the All Knowing Master of Worlds, Prosperity and Order. This for the nation's new satellite TV station, this for God's satellite; this for the epic about my valiant life, this for God's film industry; this for surveillance networks across the capital, this for God's installation people; this for primary, secondary and higher; this for God's curriculums; this for me. This for the leader of the opposition party; this for the Austrian torturer; this for the editor of the national press – or is he dead? This for the MD of Crude

Futures: all of heaven's gifts down to the cracks of their arses and I, the poor, sluttish Arab, forgoing billions to worship you: I am transparent, so transparent my flesh emerges like calves milk – I beg you, Lord, give me the recognition I need and help me calculate what is good.

Is it not charm, is it not consummate charm to slouch on silk cushions and fuck and be fucked by all the flesh dollars can buy? I am a fine apprentice, do I not learn well what you taught me? This for you, oh God.

Help me, Lord, help me – your angelic ministers defame me, they portray me as a murderer, a trafficker of toxins, a strangler of children, why is this God? I lie naked before you while they deafen you with abuse. Let me not be disagreeable to you, God, I do not compete with you, how could these packets of human flesh compete with your infinity; I am your agent, nor am I an ill partner for your gluttony and endless filth.

I do not try to be pure: I have learnt so much filth, I eat filth, I am an artist of filth, I make mounds of human bodies, sacrifices to your glory, I adore the stench of rotting peasants gassed with your technology, I am a descendant of the Prophet, Peace Be Upon Him, and you, you are God. Your angelic ministers want to eliminate me, throw me like Lucifer from the lap of your mercy, but who brought me here, oh God, let us not forget, who put me here?

In front of your beneficence, I am a naked mortal, full of awe: my ugliness is not unbearable, *surely* it is not? My nose is not so hooked, is it, my eyes so diabolical as when you offered me your Washington virgins and CIA opium. Oh, God, my ugliness does not offend you now, does it?

Your plutonium, your loans, your democratic filth that drips off your ecstatic crowds – I want them all, oh God; I want your vaseline smiles and I want your pimp-ridden plutocracies; I want your world-shafting bank; I want it shafting me now – offer me the shafting hand of redemption – Oh God, let us be dirty together, won't you?

Without you, I cannot bear to be myself, cannot, cannot bear it.

Enter Hamlet holding a pistol to Claudius's head.

Hamlet: The only way to change the geography of a conflict is to have infantry on the ground firing bullets into flesh. I am the infantryman, this is the basement that reeks of human faeces and rotting meat, my emotion is the emotion of the fighter who wants to stop an invasion; here my enemy cowers, human, alone. I see the drops of sweat glistening on your skin, I can smell your fear, I can hear you breathing, I feel your fear now: stop breathing... Stop... breathing: stop breathing!

Hamlet's conviction collapses. He returns to his desk.

Black out.

END OF ACT THREE

Act Four: Al-Maghrib – Sunset

1:

Enter Polonius.

Polonius: My Lord!

Claudius: Tell the Generals: We are alone.

Exit Claudius.

Enter Gertrude.

A bell announces the beginning of the session.

Gertrude: Hamlet, you are a threat to state security.

Hamlet: Mother, you are a threat to state morality.

Gertrude: Is it drugs?

Hamlet: Is it sex?

Gertrude: Talk to me, Child, are you collaborating with the mullahs?

Hamlet: No! It is I who ask you: do you commune with the devil, Madame? Is he by you now, enveloping you? Ha! Does the devil sit by you, Gertrude, does he whisper in your ear? Ha! Does he hold you to him and thrust his hand onto your breast, is he there?! Ha! Is he there? Is he there?

Gertrude: Leave now.

Polonius prepares to leave the desk in haste, clattering objects as he moves. Hamlet hears the clattering and shoots the pistol in the direction of Claudius's desk, killing Polonius.

Gertrude: What is this!

Hamlet: From Allah we emerge and to Allah we return. Run, blood, run across the sewers and the graves, stop up the mouths of vermin and hypocrites, the squall that begins in the East moves with mighty power over the seas. Oh, Mother, Mother, I am still so young, so young to feel this weight of heaven. Your husband is a murderer!

Gertrude: You are the murderer!

Hamlet: He murdered my father!

Gertrude: Your father died of his own failures!

Hamlet: You are with the devil! The power of the *djinn* has eaten your mind.

Gertrude: Look at you, panting! Do you find me attractive, Hamlet, is that it, do you find me irresistible? You are sick!

Hamlet: The earth spins faster in its rapture as the dawn of truth approaches. *(He strikes her.)*

Gertrude: You dare to hit me!

Hamlet: I dare more!

Gertrude: Bastard son of a bastard father!

Hamlet: God cannot forget your iniquities!

Gertrude: *(She spits on him.)* On you and on your father.

Hamlet: You have out-whored Babylon!

Gertrude: Get off me, get your hands off me.

Hamlet: God's *sharia* allows you to be married to your husband's brother only when there are no other men available to you. Will you not learn, woman?

Gertrude: I will have you stripped in the streets for this, I will open your stomach with a bread knife.

Hamlet: Rude Gertrude!

Gertrude: I will hang your balls from my balcony!

Hamlet: In the time of the Prophet it happened thus, a whore passed from King to pauper, from murderer to thief, until she found the path. Will you learn? Lewd Gertrude! In the tractions of your loins do you not think on death, woman? Has lust made you mad?

Covers her eyes and raises his weapon to her womb.

Remember Allah!
Remember Allah!
Remember Allah!

Over the loudspeaker: Verse 28, Surra 5 of the Holy Koran: ***"And never say to
your father or mother** tut, **nor hold their names in vain"**. Hamlet, upon
hearing this divine voice, is cowed and amazed. He returns sheepishly to his desk.*

Gertrude: Gertrude will never forget this shame you have poured
upon her, this stain of blood will not fade.

Exit Gertrude.

Hamlet: Oh God, I have trespassed! Beware a mother's
vengeance.

Mother forgive me.
Mother?
Mother?
Mother?
Mother?

2:

Enter Claudius.

Claudius: Terrorist, terrorist, terrorist! Hamlet, we will not let an insidious terrorist coward push our nation to the brink of collapse –[6]

Hamlet: Look around you: embargoes closing in from all sides, world leaders refuse your calls, my country's assets are frozen.

Claudius: Your terror will not dictate our policy – you are exiled!

Hamlet: So it has come to this?

Claudius: Yes. Now. Go.

Hamlet: It is a far, far better thing I do now than I have ever done. Where is it to, Uncle?

Claudius: London!

Hamlet: Ah! London! I will not be alone. I will eat little, grow thin, write tracts and become the prized animal of European liberals. Good, Uncle, good; a perfect choice. Farewell, Uncle!

Claudius: I would dismember you now were it not for the glare of the world upon us. Let their lights die down – then I'll strike, invisible.

3:

Claudius: Do you think I am a monkey?

Arms Dealer: Not at all, Claudius.

Claudius: Take this. (*Handing over a list.*)

Arms Dealer: (*Reads.*) 500 howitzers, 12 B-2's, 4 stealth's, 5 submarines, 500 centurions; 17 cruise missiles; 200 hawks; 500 sparrows; 1 million rounds of ammunition... a week?

Claudius: Don't ever tell anybody I am a monkey, or I'll have you shot, do you understand?

Arms Dealer: Perfectly.

Claudius: Shhh.

Arms Dealer: Shhh.

4:

Enter Hamlet, barefoot.

Hamlet: Peace be upon the grave dwellers.
I am ill, grave dwellers, I am ill,
sick with the lies of the living,
that have spread like shredded pieces of the night,
its end resembling its beginning.
How is the end, grave dwellers, how is it worse than the
beginning?[7]
I will pass these forty nights between you,
your bones will be my books; your skulls will be my lights,
I will hold my tongue amongst you,
and eat from the dreams of the dead.

He enters his father's grave.

5:

Gertrude: Claudius! I'm drunk!

Claudius: (*On a phone.*) I want the guard doubled on the ammunition
dump – forget the water supply...

Gertrude: How can you leave me here, I'm drunk!

Claudius: What about the reserve generators? I know that... hold
them back as long as you can... I will reward you, General.

Enter Laertes.

Laertes: The dogs of war are baying for your blood; Claudius, give me
my father!

Claudius: I have missed you, Laertes.

Laertes: Where is my father?

Claudius: Missed your ethical guidance.

Gertrude: It's a coup!

Claudius: Your loyal instinct, your strength. I can feel the sniper's aim
warming the back of my head – what has happened to you, Laertes?

Gertrude: Little Laertes is mounting a coup!

Laertes: I am waiting for your answer.

Gertrude: Tell me, Laertes, if you kill him, will you marry me?

Laertes: I'll brand you like a devil's trollop.

Gertrude: I'm not your mother, I'm your Queen!

Laertes: Give me my father!

Claudius: Your father is with me. He has lost his voice. He asks me to ask you why you have betrayed him?

Laertes: I never betrayed him.

Claudius: He asks you if he ever left you wanting for anything.

Gertrude: Raise your voice, Polonius!

Laertes: Why should I want for anything?

Claudius: Then why do you align your militias with Fortinbras? Is it for *shekels*, is it arms, is it fear? What do you lack, Laertes?

Laertes: Show me my father.

Claudius: Hamlet holds him hostage.

Laertes: Where?

Gertrude: In his grave.

Claudius: Gertrude!

Gertrude: Dead!

Ophelia: Are you recording? Can I start? In the Name of God The Bounteous, The Merciful.

Laertes: Ophelia!

Claudius: She is mad, Laertes.

Ophelia: The one who has turned me into a refugee has made a
            bomb of me.[8]
            I have tried to speak the language of women,
            I have tried to forgive, on many nights I severed my tongue
            but my silence bleeds from my mouth.
            Here I am the animal that the world forgets,
            I have tried to speak language of man
            but lying no good no change can make to it

of injustice in life
I want people outside to know this
that I will express with my body what is not
able to express politics and mighty nations
so I go to my God pure in my soul in my dignity I am pure.

Laertes: Father, can your eyes see this?

6:

Claudius and Laertes removing the body of Polonius.

Claudius: Hamlet kills Laertes's father, Hamlet drives Laertes's sister out of her mind. Have Laertes's guns fallen silent?

Laertes: What are you asking me?

Claudius: Should I smother the press, should we keep this quiet?

Laertes: Announce it! And I will announce my revenge in the plumes of smoke that raze his villages to the ground.

Claudius: Those villages are your villages, I am making you Lord of the Southern region, we'll announce it tonight. *(A bomb blast, followed by a woman's scream.)* Will you let me guide you?

Laertes: I'm listening.

Claudius: Hamlet is returning with a flock of émigrés, communists and degenerate scum that the nation spat out years ago. He claims to be the Redeemer! To raise support among the people, he'll go to the Holy Mosque to lead the Friday prayers; you will meet him there with one thousand men dressed in the nation's colours. Half accidentally, your men will trample on the holy grounds and cause such brazen offence to his zealots that they will revolt there and then with stones, with tyres, with –

Laertes: What for?!

Claudius: A third of the nation.

Laertes: A third for me and a third for my father.

Claudius: Half!

Laertes: I'll do it. And if you lie, I'll kill you.

Enter Gertrude with a scream.

Gertrude: Your sister, Laertes. She came into the palace when the sun fell into the trees. When the guards were warm and droopy like the oranges her eyes were blazing and alive, her dress swollen with the wind as if with a phantom child, with fantastic wailing she moved beyond the guards into the courtyard, a swollen angel against the black sweep of the tarmac; I went towards her and as she raised her arms as if to salute the world; a button came loose from her shirt and tittered onto the steps, I remember this button, Laertes, this little disc of mother of pearl, and leaning over to retrieve it on my way home when – no – when I was there, then in the rolling flesh in the twitching limbs and her body was a well I washed myself in: how hot it felt across my face, how hot her lungs, her intestines how hot.

No one is exempt.

Exemption is impossible.

I carry my guilt, I carry it.

But, but, but...

Am I still beautiful?

Black out.

END OF ACT FOUR

Act Five: Al-Isha'a – Supper

✠

1:

At Ophelia's desk, delegates laying flowers. Islamic prayers.

Hamlet enters in a short white thowb, with a long beard.

Hamlet: I loved her, with a noble love, and I killed him. I killed your father and mine. Yes, you can look at me now, Mother. I did this out of love. What is the death of the father, Laertes, what is it, when defeat is the very secret of our rebirth?

Gertrude: Hamlet!

Hamlet: Mourn your father's death to salute the living, but do not mourn to salute the King! I want you with me in the reshaping of our nation.

Laertes: You bastard!

Hamlet: Is this fidelity, Laertes? Standing next to the King in your father's very shoes – you are not the shadow of the dead, you are death's double! *(Laertes strikes him.)* So be it! What now? Do we saddle our horses, sharpen our swords, make prayers and prepare for *Kufa*,9 thus do we rise again? Can that be? Can it be?

The other delegates return swiftly to their desks.

Arms Dealer: Your father would be proud.

Hamlet: He's dead and you – still here?

Arms Dealer: I'm leaving. My work's done. I am happy to have been of assistance.

Hamlet: I will make you regret your assistance.

Arms Dealer: Destiny makes dark plans –

Hamlet: Get out.

Arms Dealer: However we curse and spit, kick and writhe –

Hamlet: Out!

Arms Dealer: We nudge each other towards its manifestation!

Hamlet: Out!

Arms Dealer: Fortinbras will be so pleased!

Hamlet: Depart!

Arms Dealer: Farewell.

2:

Hamlet: He who can speak without tables, without chairs, without lies let them speak. (*Silence.*) This silence will bury us all.

A bell announces the beginning of the session.

I bear witness that there is no God but Allah and that Muhammed is his messenger. I, Hamlet, son of Hamlet, son of Hamlet am the rightful heir to the throne of this nation. My rule will crush the fingers of thieving bureaucrats, neutralise the hypocrites, tame the fires of debauchery that engulf our cities and return our noble people to the path of God. Our enemies comprehend only the language of blood, for this, the time for the pen has passed and we enter the era of the sword.[10] Do not pretend amazement! Violence breeds princes and princes breed violence, that is our curse!

And may God raise the souls of his martyrs to the gardens of heaven.

All vote. Gertrude hesitates.

Gertrude: Where to this madness, Hamlet, where to?

Hamlet: No more words please, Mother, words are dead, they died on our tongues, council is the weakest form of faith, now we must mouth meaning with our flesh.

Gertrude votes. War has been declared. The bell begins to iterate.

Enter a messenger.

Messenger: The world community represented in the UN has sent you this message: that it is prepared to send peacekeeping troops to the region and organise a summit meeting chaired by disinterested political figures to discuss the differences between your parties.

Hamlet: Invite your masters to a private showing to see the dead dancing before their killers,[11] perhaps you can teach us the art of slaughter and acquittal of the slaughterer.

Messenger: You will die, Hamlet.

Hamlet: No, I hurry to the dignity of life and the eternity of death.

Exit messenger.

Claudius: History lays its greatest challenge before us. Just two hours ago, our forces –

A pre-recording (sound or video) of Claudius's address to the nation begins to play and overtakes Claudius's words in the event sphere on stage. Claudius falls silent.

Each delegate, realising what has happened, rises from his/her desk, clears away the last objects of value to them, opens the munitions box beside them,[12] takes out the weapon inside it and walks forward, listening blankly yet astutely to the speech being broadcast overhead.

As they walk forward, press reports intercut into Claudius's speech, reporting the latest developments of the civil war. Amongst these gathering mounds of information, each delegate waits for the confirmation of their own death. When they hear it, they collapse, dead. To be performed in a manner as simple and unforced as possible.

Claudius's recorded address to the Nation: Just two hours ago, our forces began an attack on terrorist positions belonging to Hamlet and his army. These continue as I speak.

This conflict began when Hamlet laid siege to our democracy, our values and our people through a brutal series of kidnappings and terrorist bombings that have killed many innocent victims and shocked the world community. Tonight this battle has been joined.

The following news reports, intercut into Claudius's address, should be broadcast in Arabic:

News Report: The streets of the capital are in flames, buildings have collapsed through the endless onslaught of air attacks from the F-16 fighter planes still loyal to the King. Meanwhile, Hamlet the Crown Prince, and leader of the People's Liberation Brigade –

Claudius's recorded address to the Nation: As I report to you, air attacks are under way against military targets within the city. We are determined to knock out his lethal, nuclear potential; destroy his chemical facilities; much of his artillery and tanks will be destroyed.

News Report: In an unconfirmed report, The Queen Gertrude has been killed whilst trying to prevent the King's tanks from surrounding her son, who is trapped inside The Grande Mosque.

Gertrude dies.

Claudius's recorded address to the Nation: We will crush the terror not with books and speeches, but with courage and good judgement and responsibility. Some may ask, why act now? Why not wait? The answer is clear: the world can wait no longer.

News Report: As the Multinational Peacekeeping Force sent by the United Nations arrived off the coast yesterday, General Laertes and Hamlet's forces were engaged in arm-to-arm combat throughout the streets. At 10 am this morning reports arrived that Laertes was struck by mortar fire and his condition is described as critical.

Laertes dies.

Claudius's recorded address to the Nation: I had hoped that when we took our decision in historic debate to exile him that would be the end of this criminal life, but I have been proved wrong, and today the world will see that error corrected.

News Report: The Army is sparing no one. Hamlet is firing mortars from the Mosque and Claudius is firing from the Palace.

Claudius dies.

Hamlet: In the name of God I have invented a curse

that writes the history of other nations in my own people's blood.

Perhaps the hardest thing is to find the courage to wake in the morning and face this landscape of ruins that are our lands.

This perception of truth too late,

is hell.

Hamlet dies.

Enter Fortinbras.

Fortinbras: Faeces, intestines and sweat. Only dead humans can smell like that. I have biblical claims upon this land, it is empty and barren and my presence here is a fact that has not been invented. It won't be easy, terrorism is not yet defeated, but the pipeline will be completed within a year, and hunger will be eradicated, the homeless will find refuge, the old will die and the young will forget, the poor will find wealth and this barren land will be seen to bloom. What we see here can never happen to us. For this is the dawn and the birth of the Greater

Is –

White noise fills the conference room censoring Fortinbras's voice. Fortinbras repeats the attempt and, each time, his voice is overwhelmed by white noise.

Iz...

Izzzz... Izzzzzzzz... aaaaaa.

Sudden silence.

With your help the future will be bright. Go, let the turrets point...
West; let the Centurions salute.

Arms Dealer enters and walks towards Fortinbras incredibly slowly.

Black out.

END

Notes

1. (p. 33) The names of each act are those of the five daily prayers in Islam. They are descriptions of mood not indicators of time.
2. (p. 42) From the Introduction to Al-Sayyid Qutb's *Milestones*.
3. (p. 52) From Robert Fisk's *Pity the Nation: The Abduction of Lebanon*.
4. (p. 62) The words are a rough translation of a Bosnian folk song.
5. (p. 63) Other capital cities used in performance:
   Baghdad?
   Too many Americans!
   Kuwait?
   Too much Democracy!
   Dubai?
   Too many Russians!
   Qatar?
   Too much freedom of speech!
   Bahrain?
   Too many tombs!
6. (p. 75) US Vice-President George Bush Snr., on visiting the site of the bombed American Marine Headquarters, Beirut, 26 October 1983.
7. (p. 76) These lines echo the reported words of the Prophet Muhammed (PBUH) upon his visit to a cemetery, during one of the last nights of his life.
8. (p. 78) The opening line is from a poem by contemporary Palestinian poet, Mahmoud Darwish.
9. (p. 81) The battle of Kufa was the first in which Muslims fought against fellow Muslims.

10. (p. 82) Osama Bin Laden in a speech broadcast by Al-Jazeera Satellite Television on 7 October 2001.

11. (p. 83) This image is from a poem by contemporary Iraqi poet, Muthafar Al-Nawab.

12. (p. 83) This stage direction is, perhaps, too directorial. In my own production of the piece, the munitions boxes referred to were brought into the conference room by each of the delegates after their meeting with the Arms Dealer. Laertes, who is the only delegate who does not meet with the Arms Dealer, picks up his father's munitions box. However, it is entirely possible to imagine this scene taking place with no munitions boxes, no movement downstage of the delegates and so on. In the same way that it is possible to imagine playing this entire text without conference desks, corridors and other paraphernalia of the conference or international summit.

مؤتمر هاملت

تأليف : سليمان البسام

النص الأصلي للمسرحية المكتوب باللغة الانجليزية والعربية

كتب المقدمة جراهام هولدرنس

"في عملـه المدهش ... أخـذ البسام قصة هاملت وأعاد صياغتهـا بإسلـوب شعـري جديد .. و النتيجة مذهلة"

صحيفة السكوتس مان .

تقع أحداث المسرحية في قاعة في مكان ما من العالم العربي. وفيها ينحت البسام اقتباسا شديد القوة والاضطراب لنص هاملت الشكسبيري، حيث تتلى حكاية قائد عربي معاصر مات لتوه، و الذي يتلاعب بدولارات النفط وبتجارأسلحة، ودعاة الديمقراطية سعيا لقمع موجات التطرف الديني التي تنمو في البلد: المسرحية تقدم هاملت كلعبة سياسية قاتلة .

غرفة الاجتماعات تلك تكشف المستور لما يسمى بـ "شفافية" السياسة المعاصرة وهي الغرفة ذاتها التي تتحول إلى ميدانًا للحرب الأهلية. المسرحية لا ترمي إلى دولة محددة، إلا أنها تقدم مزيجا من الهموم العربية التي تشغل شعوب من الخليج إلى المحيط.

هذه الطبعة مزودة بالصور من الجولة العالمية للعمل المسرحي من إخراج البسام (٢٠٠٢ – ٢٠٠٥م).

"عرض درامي محكم البناء ، يصور انحطاط المجتمع إلى التطرف والفوضى"

صحيفة ساندي هيرالد

سليمان البسام مؤلف ومخرج مسرحي كويتي. قدم مسرحيته "كليلة و دمنة، مرآة الملوك" (والتي تدور حول الكاتب عبدالله ابن المقفع) في الكويت و اليابان و بريطانيا في عام ٢٠٠٦. أما مسرحيته الفادمة المصورة لريتشارد الثالث لشكسبير فتعرض باللغة العربية مع فرقة شكسبير الملكية في بريطانيا في العام ٢٠٠٧ .

يعمل المؤلف و المخرج الكويتي بين الكويت ولندن.

بروفسور جراهام هولدرنس له مؤلفات عديدة تقدم دراسات نقدية للمسرح النهضوي والحديث.

مؤتمر هاملت

تأليف
سليمان البسام

مؤتمر هاملت

تأليف

سليمان البسام

الطبعة الأولى 2006 ©

مؤتمر هاملت : منمنمة عربية سياسية

مقدمة

بقلم : أ. د. جراهام هولدرنس

دخل شكسبير العالم العربي بشكل مدهش مبكرا في عام ١٦٠٨ وذلك خلال الرحلة الثالثة لشركة الهند الشرقية . وفي جزيرة سوقطرة الواقعة في مدخل خليج عدن، قدم طاقم مركب التنين الأحمر مسرحية هاملت لشكسبير كان عمرها أقل من عشر سنوات، وقد تم نشرها قبل خمس سنوات . كان واضحا أن قبطان السفينة وليم كيلنج William Keeling، وراعي شكسبير النبيل ساوثهامبتون قد تشاركا الاهتمام بشكسبير .
(See Holderness and Loughrey، Arabesque ،٢٠٠٦)

وسوقطرة الآن هي جزء من جمهورية اليمن ؛ أما هاملت فلا يحتاج الى تعريف. بعد انتهاء الحرب العالمية الأولى نسب اف. اس .بواس F.S.Boas الى البحرية البريطانية الفضل الريادي في نقل الدراما الشكسبيرية الى بقاع العالم.(Boas، p. ٩٥). وقد أصبحت اليمن الآن غير بعيدة نسبيا عن المملكة المتحدة، ولكن هذا الحدث الذي دخل بموجبه هاملت المنطقة على يد الإمبراطورية البريطانية الناشئة وقتها، يؤكد رأي مايكل نيل Michael Neill القاضي بأن مسرحيات شكسبير قد ارتبطت ومن البداية بمشاريع الاستعمار وبناء الإمبراطورية .
(Neill، p ١٦٨).

٢
هاملت في المسرح العربي

عاد شكسبير الى العالم العربي في أواخر القرن التاسع عشر ولكن بشكل مسرحي : أي على صورة مسرحيات مترجمة ومعدة من قبل فرق مسرحية مصرية

وعربية . وقد قدمت مسرحية هاملت للمرة الأولى في مصر عام ١٨٩٣، حيث أحبها الجمهور بميلهم الى الاستماع بقصص الأشباح و الانتقام و الجنون . وكانت الأعمال المسرحية قد استندت على الترجمات الفرنسية لشكسبير، ولذلك خضعت المسرحية لإعداد جذري، تم فيه حذف مشاهد معينة وإضافة مقاطع غنائية تصور شاعرية هاملت لأوفيليا تصويرا غزليا. وبالإضافة الى ذلك، فقد تحول الشكل التراجيدي للمسرحية الى رومانسية تاريخية ؛ فيهزم هاملت عمه ويتولى العرش حاكما بمباركة من الشبح : "لتعش حياة سعيدة على الأرض، ولتنل المغفرة في السماء". (الترجمة لتانيوس عبده، واقتبسها الشتاوي ص . ٤٤)

النهاية السعيدة للترجمة الفرنسية لهاملت ومع أنها جاءت متأثرة بالتصور التنويري الفرنسي لشكسبير، كانت في الواقع أقرب الى القصة التاريخية لهاملت منها الى مأساة شكسبير. في أواخر القرن التاسع عشر وأوائل القرن العشرين ،انتشرت مسرحية هاملت كعمل مسرحي قد خضع للإعداد وإعادة الكتابة من دون التزام بالنص الشكسبيري . وقد قدم شكسبير بحرية إعداد مشابهة لما شاهده المسرح الإنجليزي في القرن الثامن عشر ؛ حيث وكما يقول ديفيد سكوت كاستن (David Scott Kastan) :

"على خشبة المسرح . . قدم شكسبير ليس فقط بشكل معاصر، بل وأيضا قد عدل كثيرا ليتناسب مع توقعات الحضور المتمدن ...... وتحول (أي شكسبير) ... الى كاتب مسرحي معاصر و مرموق، ليتناسب مع الجو المسرحي الذي يعرض فيه" (Kastan.p ١٤) .

ويردد محمد الشتاوي - في نقده القاسي لشكسبير العرب- النقد ذاته الذي تلقاه المسرح الإنجليزي في القرن الثامن عشر :

"بشكل عام، كان الإنتاج السابق لهاملت فظا جدا، حيث ابتذلت تحفة شكسبير من أجل إرضاء المشاهدين العوام" (Al-Shitawi.p٦٤) .

الإعدادات الحرة المستقاة من النماذج الفرنسية كانت هي الأمر السائد في الثقافة العربية. فسادت في مصر ولعدة أعوام ترجمة خليل مطران ١٩١٦، عن

النسخة الفرنسية لهاملت والتي انتهت بقتل هاملت لكلاوديوس واعتلائه العرش بعد ذلك .

إن دخـول شكسبير يخ الثقافـة العربيـة لـم يكن بأي حـال مجـرد بث امبريالي واستقبـال سلبي من قبـل المستعمر، إن شكسبير، كما تقول نادية البحر(Nadia Al-Bahar) : " قد استزرع يخ التربة العربية "(-Al Bahar.p.١٣). والإستزراع لا يعني هنا محض التبادل فحسب، بل يشير الى هجرة ثقافية متبادلة تعبر الحدود، تترسخ من خلالها المادة الأدبية يخ تربة ثقافة أخرى ، وتتكيف مع المناخ السائد وشروطه . لقد تم استيعاب هاملت كما ذكر الشتاوي و "اندماجه يخ نسيج الحياة العربية المبدعة" (p.٦٠).

يخ مصر ومنذ أواخر القرن التاسع عشر قدم هاملت بترجمات متعددة ومتباينة، لم تطرح خلالها رؤية عربية الطابع أو تصور واضح لهاملت يخ السياق العربي . ويقول الشتاوي: "إن المسرحية كانت معروفة للمشاهد العربي ولكنها كانت تعد لتناسب الشروط المحلية للمسارح العربية والثقافة المحلية" . وسادت صورتان متنافرتان لهاملت، البطولي وغير البطولي :

"باستثناء العروض الأولية ... صور هاملت كبطل رومانسي يسعى لمحاربة الفساد ليموت من أجل العدالة ... عروض أخرى عربية قدمت هاملت المثقف العاجز عن مواجهة وقائع مجتمعه" (Al-Shitawi.p.٤٩) .

وتقر مارغريت ليتفن بتضاد الرؤية العربية لهاملت البطل مع هاملت المثقف، لتضع من خلال هذا قطيعة زمنية يخ تاريخ الاقتباس من هاملت يخ أواخر السبعينات . لقد ذهب هاملت الرومانسي المناضل يخ الثقافة ما بعد الاستعمارية، لتحل محله شخصيات متعددة ،جميعها ضعيفة، تعاني العجز العاطفي أمام مصيرها المرهق :

"هذه الشخصيات تنهار وسط الدموع والتوتر يخ اللحظات الصعبة ؛ تنصت بصمت الى الشخصيات الأخرى التي تجهر بأفضل ما لديها ؛ بينما تتلى مناجاتها بأفواه حفرة القبور أو حيث لا يوجد من يسمع أو يرى" (Litvin، ٢٠٠٥) .

وقد استعانت ليتفن بأعمال وإعدادات من مصر، وسوريا، وتونس لتوضيح هذا التحول :

هاملت يستيقظ متأخرا (سوريا، ١٩٨٤) ؛ فرقة مسرحية وجدت مسرحا ومثلت هاملت (تونس والأردن) ؛ الرقص مع العقارب (مصر ،١٩٨٩)؛ انسوا هاملت (عرضت في مصر عام ١٩٩٤ ،وتم نشرها في بيروت) . وقد استخدمت جميع هذه المسرحيات استراتيجيات فنية لتحدي الأنماط المسرحية التقليدية ؛ مشككة بقدرة الكلمات وحدها كوسيلة لإحداث أى تغيير. ومع ذلك فقد أبقت كلاوديوس الطاغية العربي بجبروته، بينما ظلت صورة هاملت "المثقف، العاجز أمام أوضاع بلده المزرية" (Al-shetawi.p ٤٨.)

٣
مسرحية مؤتمر هاملت

هذا الموروث المركب كان نقطة بداية في مسرحية سليمان البسام "مؤتمر هاملت" والتي قدمت أول مرة في إنجلترا في مهرجان أدنبرة الدولي، في أغسطس عام ٢٠٠٢، حيث فازت بجائزة النقاد للإبداع والابتكار في الكتابة و الإخراج . ومن ثم تم عرضها في مهرجان القاهرة الدولي الرابع عشر للمسرح التجريبي في سبتمبر عام ٢٠٠٢، لتفوز بجائزة أفضل عرض وأفضل إخراج . بعد ذلك و بتبني جهة يابانية ، قدمت المسرحية باللغة العربية وارتحلت في جولة عالمية فعرضت في استوديوهات ريفرسايد في لندن (مارس عام ٢٠٠٤)، وفي مهرجان الفنون في سنغافورة (يونية، العام ٢٠٠٥)، كما عرضت في قلعة هلسينور الدنماركية (آب عام ٢٠٠٥)،وفي مهرجانات أخرى في العالم (سيؤول، طوكيو، وارسو ،طهران) .

وقد مر العمل بإعدادات مختلفة لنص شكسبير منذ عام ٢٠٠١ ،فقد عرضته فرقة مسرح زاوم باسم : "هاملت في الكويت". وذلك في الكويت (٢٠٠١) ، وأيضا باسم "قمة هاملت" الذي عرض في مهرجان أيام قرطاج المسرحية في تونس (٢٠٠١). وكان العملان السابقان يقومان على النص الشكسبيري، أما مسرحية "مؤتمر هاملت" فقد نبذت اللغة الشكسبيرية وأعيد كتابة النص بلغة انجليزية عصرية استخدمت مضامين وأساليب بلاغية عربية الطابع عصرية

المغزى . لتقـدم المسرحية بذلك، ما وصفه المؤلف بـ "بنية ثقافية مزدوجة" (Al- Bassam ٢٠٠٣). وقد أنتج البسام هذا العمل باللغتين الإنجليزية و العربية، ويجمع هذا الإصدار، وللمرة الأولى، النصين المعتمدين لمسرحية "مؤتمر هاملت" باللغتين العربية والإنجليزية .

و ترسم مسرحية البسام مأساة السياسة الشرق أوسطية في هيكل مسرحية شكسبير : هاملت . الشخصيات الرئيسية تحمل أسماء أبطال مسرحية شكسبير وتأخذ مواقع موازية لها ولكن في إطار عالمها الشرق أوسطي المعاصر . فوالد هاملت، الحاكم السابق، قد قتله أخوه كلاوديوس بالسم واغتصب منصبه . غيرترود و أوفيليا، وبولونيوس وليارتس يلعبون أدوارهم في سياق قريب إلى المسرحية الشكسبيرية، ولكن في شكل ينسجم مع السياق العربي الإسلامي . في المسرحية يتم تهديد النظام، كما كانت الدنمارك مهددة في مسرحية هاملت شكسبير، من قبل قوات فورتنبراس المنتشرة على الحدود، وأيضا من قبل حركة "النضال الشعبي" في الداخل والتي توزع منشورات عن مقتل هاملت الأب. لكن وبينما سعى كلاوديوس في مسرحية شكسبير لحل أزمة التهديد النرويجي بالدبلوماسية، كان رد كلاوديوس في "مؤتمر هاملت" يتسم بالعنف والوحشية :

بولونيـوس: لدي ثلاثمائة رجل يعملون على مدار الساعة بجمع المنشورات . كلاوديوس : انس أمر المنشورات، أحرق مدن الصفيح جميعها —أريدها محترقة مع طلوع الفجر .

ويدعم الغرب جيش فورتنبراس " المسلح بأدوات تقدر بملايين الدولارات". وخلف التدخل الأجنبي يكمن جشع الغرب بنفط العرب إن ما يشغل كلاوديوس في الدرجة الأولى هو حماية أنابيب النفط من أي تخريب

و في مشهد مماثل لمسرحية هاملت(٣,٣) ، وبدل أن يظهر كلاوديوس الندم ويطلب الغفران، نجده يعبر عن عبوديته الخالصة للنفط والدولارات :

دولارات البترول . آه يا ربي يا رب المال، علمني معنى دولارات البترول، لا رب لي إلا أنت، خلقتني على صورتك، ألتمس الهداية منك يا من ترى كل شيء وتسمع كل شيء، رب العالمين والرخاء والقانون .

وفي نهاية المسرحية نلاحظ أن فورتنبراس يسعى لإبقاء مثل هذه السياسة وهذا الإعتقاد :

"لن يكون الأمر سهلا، فالإرهاب لم ينهزم بعد، ولكن أنابيب البترول ستكتمل خلال عام"

ويظهر الغرب في المسرحية من خلال شخصية تاجر السلاح الذي يتكلم الإنجليزية في الترجمة العربية، والذي تلعب دوره امرأة في النسخة الإنجليزية . وهذا التاجر يتحاور مع، و يبيع الأسلحة إلى كل من هاملت وأوفيليا وكلاوديوس وغيرترود وأخيرا فورتنبراس . وهو (أو هي) مستعد لإمداد الأسلحة لأي شخص يدفع ثمنها، شاملا بذلك أطراف الصراع في صفقاته . وفي النهاية نجده يتقدم ببطء نحو فورتنبراس بينما تطفأ الأنوار .

وكما أن كلاوديوس في النص الأصلي يعلم بأن عدوه الحقيقي إنما يقبع في الداخل، كذلك كلاوديوس وبولونيوس في "مؤتمر هاملت"، حذران تجاه كل أنواع التخريب والإنحراف. المعارضة والنقد يتم تأويلهما من قبل السلطة على أنهما ارهاب .وهذه التهم المفتعلة تربط حتى قصيدة هاملت لأوفيليا بمقصد إرهابي، فيرى بولونيوس في رسائل هاملت، مايدل على "رغبة الدمار الشامل و التغيير في نظام العالم" . كما يتبنى كل من أوفيليا وهاملت سمات إسلامية ويلبسان اللباس الإسلامي ليصبحان بالتالي في نظر النظام "إرهابيين". وترمز أوفيليا- كما لاحظت خوري – Yvette K. Khoury – إلى القضية الفلسطينية، حيث تموت في عملية انتحارية، بينما يقوم هاملت (بثوبه الإسلامي القصير ولحيته الطويلة) بقتل بولونيوس، وفي خاتمة المسرحية يشاهد وهو يقود جيش التحرير.

كلاوديوس : منذ ساعتين فقط، بدأت قواتنا هجومها على معاقل الإرهاب التابعة لهاملت وجيشه . والاشتباكات ما زالت تتواصل حتى حين إلقاء هذه الكلمة، بدأ هذا الصراع عندما فرض هاملت حصارا على ديمقراطيتنا، وعلى قيمنا وشعبنا من خلال سلسلة أعمال وحشية من خطف وتفجيرات إرهابية تسببت في قتل العديد من الضحايا الأبرياء وهزت المجتمع الدولي .

تجسد شخصية هاملت المعادلة بين التطرف الإسلامي والنشاط الإرهابي. وهذه المعادلة توازي كلا من رغبة هاملت بالانتقام وجنونه في المسرحية الأصلية، وكلاهما ينتهيان بحمام دموي انتقامي يستعين بمفردات وتعابير دينية الطابع[1]:

أشهد أن لا إله إلا الله وأشهد أن محمدا رسول الله

سوف أطهر هذه الأرض سأجعلها نقية، أنا أفهم، أنا فعلا أفهم، لكني سوف أطهرها من أجلك، سوف أعدها من أجلك، سوف أعدها لعودتك، ولو كلفني ذلك حياتي، سوف أنظفها ،سوف أطهرها، ستفيض الدماء، سأجعلها تفيض سيولا، أقسم برحمة أبي، وأقسم بالله .

٤
مكانة مسرحية مؤتمر هاملت في تراث هاملت العربي :

ولكن أين تقف هذه المسرحية أمام كل من الرؤية العربية الشكسبيرية و التأويلات المسرحية السائدة لهاملت في الغرب ؟ ترى مارغريت ليتفين أن البسام قد تخلى عن هاملت المثقف العاجز الذي قدم في أواخر القرن العشرين ليعيد التواصل مع الصورة الرومانسية لهاملت التي سادت المسرح العربي في السابق . فهاملت البسام حسب ما تقول ليتفين : يختلف عن الشخصية المهزومة التي صورتها المسرحيات العربية المعاصرة حول هاملت، ليستعيد هاملت بطولته التي عرضتها مسرحيات الحقبة الستينية والسبعينية من هذا القرن (Litvin٢٠٠٥).

ووفق هذا التحليل فإن البسام قد تجاوز العقدين السابقين وأعاد التواصل مع تراث عربي أقدم، إذ قسمت مسرحيته "مؤتمر هاملت" أقساما تنسجم مع أوقات الصلاة الخمسة في الإسلام، وذلك على غرار مسرحية رياض عصمت التي انتجت في دمشق عام ١٩٧٣، والتي قسمت الى ثلاثة أقسام مسماة تباعا : الحزن، الثورة، الشهادة . (انظر الشتاوي Al- Shetawi، p٤٨) .

---

1 يقصد الناقد أن المسرحية قد اقتبست العبارات الدينية كالبسملة والشهادتين في محاكاة قد تدل على الزيف الناتج من استخدام عبارات مقدسة لتبرير النزعة الدموية.

من جهة أخرى فإن صورة المجاهد الإسلامي التي يرسمها هاملت البسام لا تشبه، أو تقارن بأبطال القرن السابق. فبطل البسام على الرغم من كونه مناضلا نشطا في وجه الفساد ومحاربا من أجل العدالة كما يعرض هنا:

هاملت : إن العدو الحقيقي هنا، في القصر، بيننا .

ليارتس : لن يكون هناك من أحد نقاتل من أجله إلا إذا هزمنا فورتنبراس

هاملت : لن يكون هناك من شعب نفقده إلا إذا تخلصنا من العفن الذي يلتهمنا من الداخل

نجده بعد ذلك يتحول الى رجل براغماتي، يرفض لغتي الحوار والعقل ليهب نفسه كليا للغة العنف :

هاملت : زمن القلم ولى ودخلنا زمن السيف . كفى من كلماتك كفى !قد مل قلبي من هرائك واكتفى . والكلمات اغتصبت من معانيها الأيام . وبات اللسان أضعف الايمان، ولا يتبقى لنا سوى أرواحنا

ومن جهة أخرى، على الرغم من أن موت هاملت قد رسم دلالة واضحة للطابع الإستشهادي الإسلامي : (المجد والخلود لشهدائنا الأبرار)، إلا أن هذا لا يمثل سوى جزئية صغيرة من المشهد الدموي الأخير، حيث الإنقلاب الفاشل على الحكم، ودخول القوات الغربية ونيل فورتنبراس السلطة . وتلتف هذه الأحداث جميعها في إطار إعلامي يجسد كل ما يحمله الحدث الإعلامي من الدمج بين الموضوعية والتزييف في آن واحد . إذا كان هاملت قد طهّر الأرض، فذلك أدى إلى فسح المجال لفورتنبراس بنقل قواته اليها . الجهادية الإسلامية لم تقدم الحل، بل قدمت فقط نهاية حبكة درامية :

فورتنبراس : لدي إدعاءات ومطالبات بموجب كتب سماوية بهذه الأرض، فهي فارغة وقاحلة ووجودي بها حقيقة ليست محض خيال .

٥
الأبعاد الثقافية للمسرحية : رؤية نقدية

طالما كان هناك تراث عربي محدد في معالجة وإعداد شكسبير، كان عمل البسام يشكل جزءاً من هذا التراث . ولكن البسام، وبموجب كتابته النص باللغة الإنجليزية، يعمل في نطاق الثقافات الأنجلوفونية «الثقافة المنطوقة باللغة الإنجليزية » .

وهذه الثقافة كما وصفها مايكل نيل Michael Neill "مشبعة بشكسبير" : "إن طرق تفكيرنا حول مثل هذه المسائل المهمة كالمواطنة، والجنس gender، والفروق العرقية متأثرة وبشكل كبير به « أي بشكسبير» وبكتاباته (Neill. p١٤٨).

وقد أعلن البسام صراحة أن عمله المسرحي ينصب على خط التماس ما بين ثقافتين . إذ أنه يتكلم من منظور عربي، ولكن في الآن ذاته يوجه خطابه إلى جمهور أجنبي:

" لقد كتب النص من منظور عربي معاصر . وهو يحمل مواضيع و هموماً كثيرة تخص الوضع الحالي للعالم العربي وعلاقاته بالغرب . كما يقوم النص بتقديم هذه الأمور للمشاهد الناطق باللغة الإنجليزية . فالبناء الثقافي المزدوج لهذا النص إنما يورط الأنا بالآخر " (Al-Bassam ٢٠٠٣) .

وقد يشبه هذا الرأي ما يمكن تسميته بالهجين الثقافي الحادث عندما يتخلل الخطاب الإمبريالي في داخل ثقافة ما بعد الاستعمار وينتقل عبر الأدوات المحلية والوطنية، ليشكل خليطا مركبا . لكن يجدر الإنتباه الى أن مسرحية " مؤتمر هاملت " لا تنسجم بسهولة في أي من النماذج التي يضعها النقد ما بعد الإستعماري . إن أي كاتب يصوغ وبشكل مقصود على هامش ثقافي أو وطني، أو يتجاوز الحدود التاريخية والمحلية، إنما يكون كاتبا يسعى الى خلق توازن صعب وغير ثابت، ليجد نفسه بالتالي أمام تحديات كثيرة، وهو ما يقره البسام نفسه إذ يقول :

" بالنسبة للبعض، كانت مسرحية " مؤتمر هاملت" عملا خيانيا و مواليا للغرب، والذي ــ حسب رأي هؤلاء ــ يربط بصورة مغلوطة بين الإسلام وانتشار الإرهاب . أما بالنسبة لآخرين وهم الأكثرية و من الشباب خاصة، كانت المسرحية طرحا

ضروريا و ملحا للهموم العربية المعاصرة، تم تقديمها للغرب بنسق حضاري وانساني الطابع". (Al- Bassam، ٢٠٠٣) .

وقد تساءل حتى المعجبون من النقاد بالبسام عن حقيقة موقفه . فها هو بيتر سميث Peter J. Smith ٢٠٠٤) يسأل :

"ألا تعمل الصورة الأصولية والإنتحارية لكل من هاملت و أوفيليا على تعزيز الآراء المتطرفة التي تنشرها الصحف الصفراء ؟ (٧٤-٥). لكن سميث يعود بدوره ويتراجع عن نقده السابق ليشكك في مدى أحقية ومشروعية آرائه حول رؤية البسام : "من أنا، باعتباري الشخص غير المسلم وغير العربي ،والذي يتكلم الإنجليزية، لأقول للبسام كيف يكتب ويخرج رؤيته الخاصة ؟" (٧٥.Smith، p). وتسأل مارغريت ليتفين ذات الأسئلة حول رؤية البسام:

"لا تتعلق مسرحية البسام أبدا بالتاريخ الحقيقي لشكسبير العربي .. لقد وضع البسام نفسه كمؤلف يكتب ليس للعرب وإنما بالإنابة عنهم ،كما أنه يزيل الفوارق بين ما هو شخصي وما هو محلي ...لم ينو البسام أن يكتب مسرحية عن هاملت للمشاهدين العرب . لقد فضل عوضا عن ذلك أن يصدم مشاهديه الغربيين، وعلى الأخص الإنجليز ويقحمهم في الإثارة و "الشعور بالغرابة" .

بالنظر الى ان البسام ينوي تحويل المسرحية الى فيلم سينمائي عربي، فإن الرأي السابق لليتفين يحتاج الى إعادة دراسة . وعموما فإن هذه الردود النقدية إنما تشير الى قدرة مسرحية "مؤتمر هاملت" على خلق حوار يتجاوز الحدود الإقليمية، وهو حوار يتحدى القيود والتحفظات ويسائلها ويقتحمها .

المسرحية أيضا تقترح بديلا ضروريا وعاجلا لسوء الفهم والعنف المتبادلين . إن ما أسماه البسام بالإلتحام الثقافي cultural symbiosis الذي يبرز في مسرحيته كان مصمما من أجل تشكيل قاعدة للحوار بين الشرق و الغرب (ليس من الضروري أن يكون الحوار متساهلا أو سهلا) . إن النص المستقل عن النص الشكسبيري يخلق فضاءات أرحب للتعبير عن التجربة العربية، وهو انتقال هام جدا في صيرورة هذا العمل .

٦

العولمة في إطار مسرحية مؤتمر هاملت

بدأت كتابة مؤتمر هاملت مع تجربة العولمة، يتذكر البسام قائلا :
"كنت في القاهرة مع مخرج مسرحي عراقي منفي وفرقة مسرحية فلسطينية من
رام الله في البازار نحتسي القهوة عندما ركض صبي نحونا منشدا "الكل مرتبط/
أمريكا قربت".

لقد كان يوم الحادي عشر من سبتمبر وقد تناقلت شاشات التلفزة أخبار نيويورك.
وفي خضم زحمة هذه الليلة أستطيع تذكر كلمات أحد الممثلين الفلسطينيين: إن
الجحيم الذي لاقته نيويورك اليوم سيجلب الجحيم الى رام الله غدا " (-Al
. (٢٠٠٣ Bassam

يعد يوم الحادي عشر من سبتمبراللحظة الأهم في تاريخ العولمة، معروضا
هنا من خلال وجهات نظر مختلفة. لقد حمل إنشاد الصبي احتفالا انتصاريا
بالعالم المتقلص، وبالسهولة التي استطاع بها الإرهاب الوصول الى قلب المؤسسات
السياسية والاقتصادية في الولايات المتحدة الأمريكية. أما الممثل الفلسطيني فقد
عبر بأسى عن النتائج الإنتقامية التي ستقوم بها إسرائيل وليست أمريكا، و نحو
الشعب الفلسطيني. الأحداث في عصر العولمة إذاً لا يعيقها الزمان والمكان .

في مقالة حول يوم الحادي عشر من سبتمبر، نقل توني بلير هذه المشاعر بدقة
حيث قال أن هذا اليوم قد أعطى المعنى الحقيقي للعولمة :
"في هذا العالم، عندما ينزل الجوع والفوضى في بلد ما، تنتشر المشاكل خارجه
بسرعة . لقد كان مجرد مخيم موحش في تلال أفغانستان ما اشعل الهجوم المدمر في
قلب مركز التجارة العالمي في نيويورك (Blair ١١٩) " .

هذا هو الجانب السيء من العولمة . ولكن بنظر بلير تحمل العولمة أيضا الحل
الممكن لمثل هذه المشاكل . فالغرب يستطيع "استخدام قوة المجتمع في جلب مزايا
العولمة للجميع " (١٢١) وذلك على شكل قيم عالمية : "قيم كالحرية، وسيادة
القانون، وحقوق الإنسان والمجتمع التعددي ... قيم هي "عالمية وتستحق احترام
جميع الثقافات" (١٢٢). وآلة نشرهذه المبادئ في العالم هي الإختراق الإقتصادي

وذلك : "بزيادة التدفق التجاري، واعطاء القطاع الخاص دورا أكبر في المال العام (١٢١).

البسام بدوره قد تعمد وبشكل واضح أن تكون مسرحيته "مؤتمر هاملت" تدخلا في هذا النقاش المشحون. يقول البسام حول إشكالية العولمة :

" إن مسألة العولمة في السياسة هي أمر مخادع . كل عربي يعرف قول جورج بوش "إما أن تكون معنا أو ضدنا" والكل في الغرب يعرف رداءة صدام . هذه هي السياسة المعولمة، ولكنها لا تفعل شيئا لدفع الحوار بين الحضارات. وكل ما تفعله هو تقديم رؤى عالمية فارغة المضمون . وهنا بالضبط تصبح الثقافة والمسرح من الأهمية بمكان. فهما يسمحان بالتنوع والإختلاف، ليصبح الضعيف غير ذلك الشخص الذي يثير الشفقة، والقاسي غير ذلك المكروه . إن المسرح يتحدى الآراء التي يرتضيها العالم ويكسر مرايا السلطة . وقد فهم شكسبير هذه القوة التي للمسرح فهما جيدا". (Dent) .

العولمة اذن ليست فقط شيئا لا مفر منه، بل ويمكن أن تصبح مطلوبة، ذلك أنها السبيل الوحيد للتفاهم المتبادل وللإستقرار العالمي. كل شيء مرتبط ببعضه البعض، كما لاحظ الصبي في المقهى . والمشكلة تكمن في كيفية تطوير مثل هذه الروابط من غير عنف وصدام ؛ ومن غير وجود التفوق الغربي، وقمع الحضارات الأخرى . ولأجل تحقيق ذلك يصبح للمسرح دوره الحساس :

" إن أحداث الحادي عشر من سبتمبر والآثار السياسية التابعة لها وضحت الإرتباط اللزومي بين أقدار العرب والغرب . كل شيء مرتبط ببعضه البعض ، ومقولة صراع الحضارات اللجوجة تبسط وتغطي على ما هو مسلسل معقد من الوقائع الثقافية التي تمتد وتتداخل والتي يضمها نوع من الإلتحام المصيري (aL- Bassam،٢٠٠٣) "

وهذا مدخل مختلف تماما عن تصور توني بلير حول نشر القيم التنويرية للديموقراطية الحرة عن طريق الرأسمالية بسوقها المفتوحة. بالرغم من أن البسام لا يدافع عن التطرف الإسلامي أو الإرهاب، إلا أنه قد أظهر أنهما نتاجان لازمان من التحالف بين الاستبداد العربي و بين الآلية الإقتصادية للغرب. في

مسرحية شكسبير، وجد هاملت نفسه مدفوعا الى الإنتقام، و في مؤتمر هاملت البسام، اضطر كل من هاملت و أوفيليا الى السير في درب دموي انتحاري .

٧

ما بين عام ١٦٠٨ - عندما خرجت أصداء كلمات شكسبير من ظهر مركب "التنين الأحمر" في العالم العربي - وحتى العام ٢٠٠١، حين وجدت رؤية البسام التي لاقت القبول والترحيب في الشرق والغرب، نهضت امبراطوريات واندثرت أخرى. ولكن شيئا هاما قد تغير. ففي عام ١٦٠٨ كان شكسبير يحدث نفسه. أما في عام ٢٠٠١ فقد أصبح شكسبير موضوع نقاش عالمي. "كل شيء مرتبط" في نظام العولمة، إما من خلال العنف أو من خلال القبول بالعلاقات المتبادلة والإرتباط المتبادل. ومسرحية "مؤتمر هاملت" إنما تفتح باب الحوار على أرضية الوفاق المشترك .

تنويــه
أود أن أنقل شكري وامتناني الى كل من مارغريت ليتفين، و بيفيت خوري وبيتر سميث وأخيرا سليمان البسام بما قدموه لكتابة هذه المادة.

"معاً على الدرب..."
مقدمة المؤلف سليمان البسام

.

" – بيروت ؟ فيها الكثير من الملشيات.

– دمشق ؟ فيها الكثير من البعثيين.

– القاهرة ؟ فيها الكثير من العبثيين.

– السخرية؟ أص!!! هناك الكثير من الدبلوماسيين !"

غالباً وقبل كل عرض للمسرحية ﰲ البلاد الغربية، يخضع هذا الجدول للعواصم العربية و ملامحها الساخرة (ﰲ الفصل الثالث) لتغييرات مستعجلة ﰲ أجنحة خشبة المسرح، وذلك حسب هوية السفير العربي الذي يصادف أن يكون جالسا ﰲ صالة العرض، والذي يُخشى أن يرى ﰲ تلك الجمل الفكاهية، التافهة إساءة أخلاقية له و لوطنه !!

يبدو أن المسرح الساخر ﰲ عالمنا العربي ينتصر بسهولة على المسرح السياسي الجريء أو التراجيدي كمصدر للفضيحة الوطنية – الأمر الذي يؤكد لنا انتصار الهزل على المعنى!

.

أحد المشاهد الماثلة ﰲ ذهني تتعلق بعرض مسرحية مؤتمر هاملت ﰲ ليلة مثلجة ﰲ طهران . كنا نستعد للعرض، عندما أخبرونا وقبل أقل من ساعة على بدءه، أن المسرحية لا بد وأن تعرض أولا على الرقابة.

كنت أتوقع حدوث ذلك، لكن العقدة كانت ﰲ وجود خمسمائة مشاهد تجمهروا أمام المسرح الكبير ﰲ طهران، منتظرين بفارغ الصبر أن تفتح لهم الأبواب لمشاهدة العرض، وسيضطرون للانتظار ساعتين أخريين تحت زخ الثلج المتساقط، لينتهي الرقيب من رؤية العرض !! وبالفعل قام منظموا العرض بالاعتذار لجمهور يكسوهم الثلج بينما كنا نؤدي المسرحية أمام أرتال

من المقاعد الفارغة إلا من مشاهد وحيد هو موظف من إدارة الرقابة يلبس العمامة.

اعترض الرقيب على تلاوة القرآن التي علت في المشهد الأول من الفصل الرابع لتمنع هاملت من إفراغ مسدسه في رحم أمه. دخلنا في نقاش متحضر يتناول المعنى والمغزى المقصود من استخدام هذه الدلالة الدينية، حاولت من خلاله توضيح قيمة هذه الدلالة التي تعتبر، وبلا شك، الدليل الأوضح على نبذ الإسلام للعنف والارهاب. عندها هز الموظف رأسه — وقد كان رجلاً متديناً ومثقفاً — ليسمح بدخول حشود المشاهدين الذين غطى الثلج أكتافهم.

.

– "شغب، يا رجل؟ أهناك باب خلفي؟"

في القاهرة كان عرضنا على مسرح صغير، ومع هذا فقد حضر جمهور غفير جذبه ما قيل بشأن المسرحية والقنبلة السياسية التي تفجرها، فبيعت التذاكر واصطفت أرتال من المتحمسين للعرض. لكن صدف أن حضر عشرة من أعضاء لجنة التحكيم الأجانب يرافقهم عشرة مترجمين، تبعهم موكب من سيارات المرسيدس التي كانت تنقل سفيراً أجنبياً وضيوفه، وكان أن سرت الشائعات التي ترى أن المسرحية لم تكن سوى رقصة امبريالية خاصة، فهبت الفوضى والشغب بين المتجمعين الذين حاولوا كسر أبواب المسرح الزجاجية، وحضرت الشرطة التي اعتقلت سبعة من الثائرين، عندها انسل السفير بسرعة من خلال الباب الخلفي للمسرح. ولتهدئة النفوس الهائجة طلب منا منظمو العرض أن نقوم بعرض ثان للمسرحية عند منتصف الليل، فكان أن عاد المتحمسون للحضور ليلا وقد استمتعوا بأفضل عرض قمنا به لمسرحية مؤتمر هاملت (النسخة الانجليزية).

.

اتهمني أحد نقاد المسرح العرب، في تجمع عام في الكويت، بأنني تلقيت في مسرحية مؤتمر هاملت دعماً سريا من منظمة اسرائيلية تحتجب خلف هيئة يابانية راعية، بغية توجيه موجة معادية للعرب تحت اسم عمل كلاسيكي. ومن

زيادة العجب أن ارتأى هؤلاء العملاء المتآمرون أن تقديم النص باللغة العربية سيزيد من مصداقية النص ومادتة المعروضة !

.

بما يخص مونولوج فورتنبراس في اللحظات الأخيرة من المسرحية، من الممكن أن يتلو فورتنبراس عبارته كلها في اللغة العبرية كبديل مقبول يرسم هذه اللحظات ومغزاها.

.

بالنسبة للديكور، لا أرى ضرورة أن يكون ديكور المسرحية على غرارالمؤتمربسجاده الأحمر المفروش والمقاعد والطاولات التي تعلوها الميكروفونات وعلب المياه المعدنية، يمكن للعمل أن يقام وبصورة درامية عالية على مسرح فارغ. أما "الفضاء التام" الذي يشير إليه هاملت في الفصل الثالث، فهو فضاء أشبه بفضاء المجلس (ملتقى الرجال في البيوت الخليجية) حيث يحيط الرجال جلوساً أطراف الغرفة، بينما يكون المركز فارغاً تماماً . إن تصميم مجلس الأمن في نيويورك يشبه تصميم المجلس العربي وإن كانت حلقته دائرية.

.

الغلو الديني يغزو المسرحية من جميع جوانبها. نجدها في قناع الحاكم، وفي غضبة المظلوم، وخطة الثائر و بالنتيجة الشك والحوار يتلاشيا عن الوجود.

.

فيما يتعلق بالزمن، فإن أحداث الفصل الأول من المسرحية تقع في يوم واحد، وبعد ذلك تتوالى الأحداث في فيض زماني يضيق ويتسارع عند الدخول في الفصلين الرابع والخامس ، لذا فإن أسماء الفصول التي تعود إلى الأوقات الخمس للصلوات، ترمز إلى المزاج والحالة النفسية أكثر من دلالتها الزمنية.

.

الأحداث السياسية المعاصرة تلوح كطيف ضبابي يكاد لا يرى، يختبئ خلف ستارة المسرح.

.

تاجرالأسلحة قد يكون شبحاً، قرينا، حفار قبور، رجلاً، امرأة أو حتى طفلاً.

.

لقد كتبت النص ألأصلي بالإنجليزية، لكن تحويله إلى نص عربي قد أحدث تحويراً في النص الأصلي يمكن رصده، على سبيل المثال، في مناجاة هاملت " السلام علـىيكم يا أهل القبور..." (الفصل الرابع)، وفقرة "حصان الحرب" (الفصل الثالث). هذان المشهدان تحديداً يحملان دلالات ثقافية عربية بحتة، فخطاب "أهل القبور" يوحي بخطاب النبي محمد (ص) في آخر أيامه، أما فقرة "حصان الحرب" فهي محاكاة ساخرة ترسم ولعنا بأمجاد الأمة الغابرة.

.

هناك أيضاً فروق بالغة الدلالة من الناحية الثقافية لما يتعلق بالنصيين العربي والإنجليزي، تتجسد خصوصاً في مونولوج كلاوديوس "دولارات البترول" حيث يقول النص الإنجليزي: "ربي، ربي، علمني معنى دولارات البترول"، بينما نجد النص العربي يتلو: "ربي، رب المال، علمني معنى دولارات البترول". هنا نجد أن النص الانجليزي يضع نفسه في إطار لغة دنيوية في الوقت الذي يعمل فيه النص العربي ضمن أطار الدلالات الدينية.

.

ترجم النص إلي العربية بمساعدة الكثيرين. وأنا أقدم شكري للمترجمين والممثلين والأصدقاء الذين ساهموا بتقديم النصح والنقد والإضافة الغنية للترجمة. النص الإنجليزي – وهو النص الأصلي – ما كان ليكتب دون مساهمة ودعم محررة النص، زوجتي، جورجينا. كلمة شكر أخيرة لجميع الأصدقاء والأخوة والزملاء الذين ساندوني في هذا العمل حتى خرج بالصورة التي انتهى إليها.

سليمان البسام
الكويت، 2006

مسيرة العمل

طاف هذا العمل ومنذ البدء بعرضه دولاً عديدة وشارك في مهرجانات عدة ومنها:

- تم تقديم العمل باللغة الانجليزية لأول مرة في أغسطس ٢٠٠٢، ضمن فعاليات مهرجان أدنبرة الدولي، انتاج فرقة Zaoum Theatre .

- حاز على جائزة نقاد المهرجان (Fringe First Award) عن الابتكار في التأليف والإخراج..

- حاز على جائزة أفضل عرض وجائزة أفضل إخراج في مهرجان القاهرة الدولي للمسرح التجريبي ٢٠٠٢ .

- حاز على جائزة دولة الكويت التشجيعية للمسرح عام ٢٠٠٤ .

- وفي نسخته العربية تم تقديم مؤتمر هاملت في مهرجان طوكيو الدولي في اليابان – فبراير ٢٠٠٤ .

- شارك في مهرجان شكسبير العالمي – مدينة باث البريطانية مارس ٢٠٠٤.

- عُرض العمل على المسرح (Riverside Studios) في لندن .

- شارك في مهرجان سيئول الدولي في كوريا الجنوبية – ٢٠٠٤ .

- شارك في مهرجان Spotkania في وارسو في بولندا عام ٢٠٠٤ .

- شارك في مهرجان فجر في جمهورية ايران الإسلامية يناير ٢٠٠٥.

- شارك في مهرجان سنغافورة الدولي للمسرح يونيو ٢٠٠٥ .

- شارك في مهرجان هاملت السنوي وعرض في الهواء الطلق في قلعة هاملت التاريخية في هلسنيور – الدنمارك أغسطس ٢٠٠٥ .

وقد قدم هذا العمل لأول مرة في اللغة العربية بتاريخ ١٤-٢-٢٠٠٤
وتكونت فريق التمثيل من الأعضاء التالية

- كلاوديــوس : نقولا دانيال

- جيــرتـروود : أمانه والي

- هـامـلـت : كفاح الخوص

- بـولـونيــوس : مناضل داوود

- لايـارتيــس : بشار عبدالله

- أوفيلـيــا : مريم علي

- تاجر السلاح : ناجل باريت

أمامنا ست طاولات خاصة بالمؤتمرات، مجهزة بكاميرات، وبلوحات الأسماء ومصابيح مكتبية. وفي وسط خشبة المسرح، قبر مشيد من صخور. استهلال (مقدمة موسيقية). يدخل أعضاء المؤتمر بطابور جنائزي وكل منهم يحمل قطعة من أشلاء جثة هاملت الأب ويهذي أثناء وضعه القطعة بالقبر. يخرج كلاوديوس بأقصى سرعته ويتبعه كلاوديوس .

الفصل الأول - الفجر

١ .

(حوار ما قبل - الجلسة : عبر الميكروفونات ، سريع وخافت.)

جيرتروود : لِمَ وجهك مسّود ، هاملت ؟

هاملت : لا بد انه السفلس ماما ، لقد عاشرت كثيرا من العاهرات اليوم .

جيرتروود : أتمزح ؟

هاملت : ابدا! العاهرات اليوم أكثر مما كانوا أيام والدي.

جيرتروود : هاملت!!؟

هاملت : عليك أن تخرجي إلى الشارع ، ماما ، وترين البيوت المضاءة بالنيون : مواخير مواخير.

لايارتيس : أهلا بعودتك ، مولاي هاملت ، يؤسفني موت والدك ، عظّم الله أجرك.

هاملت : عظم الله إضاءتك ، لايارتيس ، ومواخيرك !

لايارتيس : مولاي!

هاملت : لا لا أنا أقدر لك ذلك يا لايارتيس ، لقد كان أباك مواليا جدا

لوالـدي، وانـي اعتمد اعتمادا كاملا على إخلاصك التام لنهجنا.

بولونيوس: إن صاحب الرهبة والعظمة، القائد الأعلى للقوات المسلحة، قائد الجو، والبر والبحر، الرئيس المنتخب لمجلس النبلاء يلفت انتباهكم الكريم إلى أن الجلسة قد بدأت.

(يُعزف عبر المكبرات الصوتية النشيد الوطني ويقف الجميع)

(يدخل كلاوديوس)

كلاوديوس: بسـم الله الرحمن الرحيم.

(صوت جرس ينبه لبدء الجلسة)

بموجب مرسوم منـي تم زرع عشرة آلاف نخلة وافتتاح حديقتين عامتين تخليدا لذكرى أخي. (تصفيق) إن وقت العزاء قد انتهى. اليوم ينبلج الفجر نحو خصوبة اكبر، وكطائر الفينيق الذي ينهض من سرير الرماد البارد يومض بألسنة اللهب – تنهض زوجتي نافضة يدها من يد أخي الرمادية، ووجنتاها رطبة بالدموع ومبللة بندى التغيير، لتشاركني حفل التتويج: لقد طلع الفجر على شعب هذه الأمة : سوف تبدأ اليوم الديمقراطية الجديدة ! (يصفق المجلس). الأمة تصفق وأنا اصفق للأمة! (يصفق المجلس) إننا نركب قمة موجة هائلة، ولدت من إرادة الشعب والضرورة التاريخية. أنا لست قائدا للشعب: أنا خادمه! (تصفيق) هاملت؟ أنت لا تصفق؟ هاملت؟

هاملت: انه الحّرمليكي، يخرج الـدود من قلب الصخر الجلمود وتحت طبقة عطورنا، أنا-

كلاوديوس: لا أحد يزيد حزنه عن حزنك، هاملت.

هاملت: أنا مزكوم برائحة العفن النتنة!

كلاوديوس: أنت كئيب، والعالم من حولك يفي احتفال وتحزن بينما الآخرون مبتهجون، إن تعويذة الحزن تبقى كالوصمة على الديمقراطية ما مضى قد مضى، ومن مات قد مات، وما يتعفن سيتعفن.

هاملت: سأوفر عليك مشاعري. إن دراستي في انتظاري، ورحلتي الليلة.

كلاوديوس: إن قوى الشر الخفية تحيط بنا من كل جانب، منشورات الأعداء تنتشر كالفئران في جحورنا، جنود فورتنبراس مسلحة بمعدات أجنبية بملايين الدولارات يصطفون على حدودنا، لو كانت المدينة أكثر هدوءاً لكنت سمعتهم يتنفسون، ولما غادرت الليلة.

جيرتروود: هاملت أنا أمك. لطالما كان وجودك في الخارج مصدر نزاعات بيننا، ولقد غيرتك بالفعل: لقد ارتأينا أنا ووالدك أن نبعدك عن الدوائر النابضة بالحماقة والجنون.

هاملت: لأكون أقرب إلى الأسرّة النابضة بالخزي والعار.

جيرتروود: إن الدولة تبكي معك، هاملت، إن جروحها مفتوحة، وتحتاج إلى وجودك الشافي. لا تسّود ذكرى والدك بشوقك للرحيل. لا تغرز خناجر في قلب أمك الدامي – أبقى معنا هاملت.

(يتم التصويت من قبل جميع أعضاء المؤتمر ما عدا هاملت)

هاملت: عندما نزلت من الطائرة شممت رائحتها بين حرس الشرف، في عناقه وعلى يديه، على رقبته وعلى ظهره. انه يدخلها، و يسترخي عليها و يتحمم بها- ذاك القلب الدامي، يا لدم هذا القلب، يا لكرم نزيفه المفضوح المسفوح يدخلها مرة وثانية وأخرى وأخرى! سأبقى... أبقى... لأبقى!

(يصوت هاملت)

بولونيوس: بالإجماع!

كلاوديوس: إن تضامننا المجيد يبارك أول اجتماع لمجلس هذه الأمة. فليعرف الأعداء إن امتنا متحدة، فليتربص بنا فورتنبراس على حدودنا، أنا أعلن عن ثلاثة أيام عطلة وطنية احتفالا بديمقراطيتنا الجديدة.

(جرس تنبيه لنهاية الجلسة)

بولونيوس: هيا، فليحضر جميع الوزراء، هناك مؤتمر صحفي يعقبه حفل

استقبال والكثير من الصور في إنتظارنا.

(يغادر الجميع ما عدا هاملت وأوفيليا).

٢ .

(صلوات عن بعد من أنحاء عديدة.)

(تدخل أوفيليا إلى مكتب هاملت خلسة.)

هاملت : لماذا تتجسسين علي ؟

أوفيليا : أنا انظر اليك.

هاملت : و أنا انظر اليك.

أوفيليا : سأذهب إذاً.

هاملت : لا، لا – أوفيليا.

أوفيليا : أنا هنا.

هاملت : مضى زمن طويل .

أوفيليا : ثلاثة مواسم صيفية ... لقد حصلت على أشرطتك، أشكرك.

هاملت : أشرطتي؟

أوفيليا : إني أحفظها جميعا عن ظهر قلب «أوفيليا عندما ينهار العالم وتسقط السموات»

هاملت : كان عالما مختلفا وقتها.

أوفيليا : و أنا ؟

هاملت : أنت امرأة الآن.

أوفيليا : ألن تنظر إليّ ؟

هاملت: الآن ؟

أوفيليا : لم لا ؟

هاملت : ليس الآن – سوف افعل، سوف افعل، أنا أتشوق إلى النظر إليك، التحديق بعينيك، والأرتواء بطلعتك، لكن ليس الآن. لا استطيع . قد يكون بسبب الحر، فدمي ليس معتادا على هذا الحر، دمي ليس ما اعتاد أن يكون عليه أوفيليا أنا فعـلا احبك، من صميـم قلبي وبكل كياني. اذهبي الآن (يكتب) عبر الليل اللامتناهي الذي ينتظرنا.... وحدك بعينيك أل.......

(تعبر النفاثات فوق الرؤوس.)

٣ :

(في أحد الممرات)

بولونيوس : لدي ثلاثمئة رجل يعملون على مدار الساعة بجمع المنشورات.

كلاوديوس : أنسَ المنشورات، احرق مدن الصفيح -جميعها – أريدها كلها محترقة مع طلوع الفجر.

(تدخل جيرترووود)

جيرترووود : ما هو الجدول للغد ؟

بولونيوس : الإفطار مع الروس، مؤتمر صحفي، ثم افتتاح البرلمان الجديد. هل ستكون سيدتي حاضرة معنا ؟

جيرترووود : طبعا.

(جرس تنبيه لبدء الجلسة)

(تعود اوفيليا إلى طاولتها و بقية الأعضاء يدخلون مكاتبهم)

كلاوديوس : ماذا تبقى لهذا اليوم، بولونيوس ؟

بولونيوس : ابني، يا مولاي، يطلب إذنك بالسماح له بمغادرة المدينة.

كلاوديوس : لماذا ؟

لايارتيس : للانضمام لصفوف المدافعين الشجعان عن استقلال امتنا.

كلاوديوس : جيد، إن شابا مثله في حاجة إلى بعض الحركة. فليتمركز في الجنوب، أمام فورتنبراس ليدير مناورات الميليشيات.

لايارتيس : هذا شرف عظيم يا مولاي.

كلاوديوس : سوف اجعل منه جنرالا.

بولونيوس : مولاي !

كلاوديوس : لاشيء كثيراً على ابن بولونيوس.

بولونيوس : أنا على ولاء لك للأبد.

كلاوديوس : أشكركم جميعا على إخلاصكم. إن الوقت ليس معنا ولا هو ضدنا، إن أعداءنا يقظون، أنهم يخططون بينما نحن نغط في النوم. تصبحون على خير جميعا.

(جرس نهاية الجلسة.)

(خروج اوفيليا، لايارتيس وهاملت).

جيرترووود : لدي اقتراح... يتعلق بأوفيليا.

بولونيوس : ماذا فعلت ؟

جيرترووود : لايارتيس سيغادر . وستصبح هي وحيدة تماما.

بولونيوس : ان لديها العديد من الهوايات، وهي عازفة بيانو ممتازة، وتقرأ

بنهم، تركب الخيل بانتظام، وتتحدث الفرنسية والألمانية والتشيكية.

كلاوديوس: إنها رائعة الجمال.

جيرتروود: بما أن هاملت سيمكث معنا وقتا طويلا: أوفيليا عرضة للخطر.

بولونيوس: هل تشكين بابنتي من أي ناحية؟

جيرتروود: أنا امرأة بولونيوس، وأشعر بوجود بذور الفضيحة قبل انتشارها في الهواء. كما إني أم و زوجة. ابني يميل إلى ابنتك تلك التي تتحدث الفرنسية، تركب البيانو، وتعزف الخيل، وهما في عمر مناسب: واقترح تزويجهما، كلاوديوس؟

كلاوديوس: وما علاقة هذا بالديمقراطية الجديدة؟

بولونيوس: بالعكس يا مولاي، سيكون ذلك أحد رموزها !

كلاوديوس: ربما سيلهي ذلك الصحافة؟

بولونيوس: إن الشعور بالمسئولية المشتركة، يا مولاي، قد يساعد الأمير هاملت في التغلب على سلبيته تجاه الأوضاع الجديدة.

كلاوديوس: إن الزواج قد يشغله عنا.

بولونيوس: سيدتي، إن بيتنا ليس بجديد على الولاء، لقد ربط بيننا الدم والشرف عبرالقرون إن ذلك سيسعد ابنتي.

(تصويت)

بولونيوس: بالإجماع!

جيرتروود: ممتاز.

بولونيوس: رائع.

كلاوديوس: سيضيء المستقبل لنا على الدوام. نخب الديمقراطية الجديدة!

بولونيوس و جيرترود: نخب الديمقراطية الجديدة !

(تسرع جيرترود الى الخروج)

كلاوديوس: مدن الصفيح، بولونيوس.

بولونيوس: سأعطي الأوامر ببدء الحرق حالا. (يخرجان)

4 :

(يدخل لايارتيس، و بيده حقيبة عسكرية.)

أوفيليا : إلى الجبال؟

لايارتيس: نعم.

أوفيليا : سوف تموت، وسيرسلون لي صورتك و انت تتدلى من شجرة.

لايارتيس: أنا لا أجيد الديبلوماسية.

أوفيليا : انتظر لبضعة أيام فقط ، ستهدأ الأمور.

لايارتيس: لاشي سيهدئ فورتنبراس إلا رصاصة في رأسه. انظري إلي : سأشتاق إليك. عيناك، أوفيليا، عيناك... إنهما ليستا الحجرين الكريمين البريئين كما اعتادتا أن تكونا، لقد اختلط بهما لون آخر. بريق باهت، أو، أو اهتياج ضئيل، أو، أو، ألم ؟ هناك الم في عينيك، اوفيليا، الم الشوق، اشتياق الحقول البكر للمحراث؟ عندما يستلقي العالم خائفا في سريره، هل تسكبين المسك و العنبر على جسدك وتتحركين مع النسيم، أعلم انك تفعلين. ولكن ليس لهذا وجدت القصور والملوك، أليس كذلك؟ لماذا وجدوا ؟ للأسر، للغزو، للسلب، لبث الفرقة، للاجتياح، اسمك البكر، فخذاك البكر، سمعتك البكر و جنسك البكر. اسمك مسنبل على السيف الملكي، ألقابنا مرشرشة بالسيل الملكي،

وشقيقتي أراها مكوّمة على الأرض بين الوعود المنفجرة وعبوات الذهب المحترقة!! أبدا، أوفيليا، أبدا! روضي هذه الرغبة في عينيك، روضيها، قبل أن أروضها لك.

(يدخل بولونيوس)

بولونيوس : الجنرال لايارتيس !!

(يؤدي لايارتيس التحية العسكرية ويخرج)

أوفيليا : لا تتركني!

(بولونيوس يقود أوفيليا من مكتب لايارتيس إلى مكتبها)

بولونيوس : أبلغوني انك والأمير هاملت كنتما متواريين في بساتين الفاكهة عند الغسق أم أن ذلك كان قرب المسبح، أين تتواريان بالضبط ؟

أوفيليا : نتمشى أحيانا عند الغسق قبل صلوات المغرب.

بولونيوس : لا تمشي عند الغسق، ولا تمشي في الليل، لا تمشي عند الفجر و لا تمشي في المساء. أريد أن اسمع صوت خطواتك في كل لحظة، ضمن مدار سمعي، ضمن دائرة حبي اللامتناهي، حبي يحدد حدود عالمك: لا تمشي خارجه إلى ما وراء الهاوية، حيث لا تسمع خطاك وبكاءك . كم الساعة الآن ؟

أوفيليا : نحو منتصف الليل.

بولونيوس : اذهبي إلى النوم يا صغيرتي، قد تكون هذه الليلة مضطربة.

هاملت : فلتسقط السموات ولتلتهب البحار، ولينهار هذا العالم المادي، ولتجول الحيوانات المتوحشة في المدن ولتوأد البنات دونما ذنب اقترفن، ولتستعر نيران جهنم ولتقترب الجنة و ليفر المرء من أخيه ومن أمه وأبيه إن الأبرار لفي نعيم وإن الفجار لفي جحيم. أبي حياتي بين يديك: لا أملك ذرة خير، غرست في حياة فاسقة، ابعدني عن الجنون، ألهمني فأهتدي، ألهمني فأهتدي.. من هناك ؟ من أنت ؟

تاجر السلاح: صديق . عفوا أنا-

هاملت: عرفتك! ماذا تريد ؟

تاجر السلاح: أزعجتك. سأذهب.

هاملت: أبق.

تاجر السلاح: احتجت هواء نقيا. صعب التنفس في هذا الفندق.

هاملت: انها الحرائق، لقد اشعلوا الحرائق.

تاجر السلاح: لقد كان والدك رجلا عظيما، تكدر العالم بفقدانه.

هاملت: أنت أمريكي ؟

تاجر السلاح: (مقتبسا) "بحار الجاهلية تلتهم العالم، وقلاع السلطة من مكة إلى القدس، من القدس إلى الأمريكيتين، والإنسان على حافة كارثة عظيمة."

هاملت: هذه كلماته هو ! من أين أتيت بها ؟

(تاجر السلاح يناوله منشور أخضر اللون).

هاملت: لا أستطيع أن أرى - إلي بالضوء ! (يمسك له قداحة. يقرأ) "سرّب الطبيب الشرعي أدلة تشير إلى ان القائد العظيم قد تم قتله. لقد توقف قلبه بسبب نيترات الصوديوم التي تم حقنها في أذنه بواسطة إبرة، تقنية اغتيال تستخدم عادة من قبل المخابرات السريّة تحت رئاسة شقيقه وقاتله كلاوديوس !! أين وجدت هذه؟

تاجر السلاح: إنها في كل سكة.

هاملت: (يواصل القراءة) "بينما ابن الملك الراحل هاملت يواصل حياته الماجنة، مقامرا يبدد ملايين الأمة على صالات اللعب في أوروبا"- يا الهي! أموال الشعب الشعب -ضوء ! " ستنتقم جبهة النضال الشعبية لهذا القتل المقزز ولن ترحم أولئك الذين ينتحبون ويندبون، ينتحبون ويصّرون أسنانهم، لقد وجدت

قوى الشـر الامبريالية وكيلا طوعيا لها يخ شـخص كلاوديوس !!

(يحرق تاجر السلاح المنشور و ينسحب بينما تمر النفاثات صارخة فوق الرؤوس، ومئات المنشورات تسقط من السماء).

هاملت: زد جبـروتك وحنقك الإلهي المقدس ضد الشيطان ذي القرنين الذي يلوث أرضنـا والشيطان الأكبر الذي يستعبد شعبنا والعالم !! ولن يهدأ لنـا حتى تنفذ مشيئة الله، لن يهدأ لنـا حتى تنفذ مشيئة الله!.

(يجمع مجموعة من المنشورات و يخرج)

٦ :

(الأعضاء نائمون على مكاتبهم. يدخل هاملت إلى مكتب اوفيليا حاملاً مئات المنشورات)

هاملت: (يريها المنشورات وينهار على الأرض) اغتيالاً مات أبي - اغتيالا، يا اوفيليا!!

أوفيليا: أنا معك.

هاملت: كوني معي. احضنيني.

أوفيليا: احبك - احبك.

(نسمع من بعيد أغنية (أهواك) لعبد الحليم حافظ بينما تطفأ الأنوار)

الفصل الثاني - الظهر

١ :

(اوفيليا، وحيدة، مرتدية غطاء على رأسها، باكية على مكتبها)

(يدخل بولونيوس).

بولونيوس: (على مكتبه) اليوم يوم جميل جدا، يوم مليئ بالانطباعات الايجابية، كلمات مذهلة، معلومات شفافة، وأريد منك أن تتقني دورك الإعلامي، يا أوفيليا، ما هذا ؟ ما الذي ترتدينه بحق الجحيم (يمشي بخفة باتجاهها ويسحب غطاء رأسها) مـا هـذا؟

(تبدأ اوفيليا بجمع المنشورات لمحاولة اخفائها عن بولونيوس)

أوفيليا : أنا مرتاحة أكثر هكذا.

بولونيوس: تبدين كإرهابية – هل تعرفين كم عدد المصورين في الخارج؟

أوفيليا : ليلة أمس

بولونيوس: ليلة أمس، مـاذا ؟

أوفيليا : هاملت.

بولونيوس: هاملت؟ !

أوفيليا : (مرتبكة) لقد احتاج لبعض المساعدة في خطبته، لكن كلمته لم تكن منطقية، تعرف، القنابل أخذت تسقط طوال الليل والنيران اشتعلت طوال الليل وانقطعت الكهرباء حوالى الثالثة. لقد كانت ليلة سيئة. هذا كل ما في الأمر.

بولونيوس: (يعثر على منشورات جبهة النضال الشعبي) من اين حصلت على هذه؟

أوفيليا : لا أدري.

بولونيوس: من أين حصلت على هذه يا أوفيليا؟

أوفيليا : قلت لك لا أدري.

بولونيوس: أجيبيني!

أوفيليا : هو، أحضرهم لي.

بولونيوس: لقد زاد الأمر عن حده كثيرا، اوفيليا. أتمنى فقط أن اتمكن من إنقاذك من السقوط. هيا معي . هيا، هيا. (يلمح هاملت باحثاً عن مستندات في مكتب كلاوديوس) هاملت ! هاملت!

(يخرج هاملت راكضاً ويلحق به بولونيوس)

(تطفأ الأنوار).

٢ :

تاجر السلاح: سموكم ! السلطة تليق بكم، تبدو كزعيم .

كلاوديوس: ما كنت أتوقعك بهذه السرعة.

تاجر السلاح : من أصبح أفلح.

كلاوديوس: والدم يجلب الذباب.

تاجر السلاح : بز.. بز.. كلود .

كلاوديوس: اصمت!

تاجر السلاح: صدقت. ممرك شديد الصدى، عليك أن تزينه بالتماثيل، مجسمات لأعداءك المدحورين، مثلاً خوازيق من العاج،الأبنوس- أعرف نحاتة محترفةً إذا أحببت.

كلاوديوس: الى متى ستبقى معنا؟

تاجر السلاح: طالما يرحّب بي.

كلاوديوس: نحن نعد للحرب. ليس من مصلحتك البقاء هنا طويلا.

تاجر السلاح: أنا أقوم برحلة صغيرة ـفي المنطقة. لقد اتصل بي بالأمس، كان منزعجاً جدا كوني لم أزره بعد، وأنت تعرف كم يبالغ ـفي عتابه: " أيها المنافق الوغد، لقد وعدتني بكذا، وكذا " .

(يضحك)

كلاوديوس: من هو؟

تاجر السلاح: فورتنبراس!

(وقفة)

كلاوديوس: أرجو أن تكون مرتاحا ـفي اقامتك؟

تاجر السلاح: ...

كلاوديوس: سنخصص لك جناحاً!

تاجر السلاح: ذاك الرجل طموح جـدا، متطلع للغاية، عصري لأقصى الحدود.

كلاوديوس: سأبعث لك صندوقاً من ما تحبه؟ - المحار؟ البرحي؟

تاجر السلاح: ها؟

كلاوديوس: يسعدني أنك معنا.

تاجر السلاح: أنا أسعد.

كلاوديوس: سنقيم لك حفلة.

تاجر السلاح: لا.

كلاوديوس: بلى. وستكون حفلة عظيمة. أريدك أن تقابل وزرائي جميعهم.

تاجر السلاح: لم لا؟

كلاوديوس: غدا – هذا المساء. سأرتب الأمر. والآن أرجو أن تعذرني يفتتح البرلمان الجديد خلال (ينظر إلى ساعته)

تاجر السلاح: ساعتان و اثنتا عشرة دقيقة – اعرف. فرصة سعيدة.

(يخرج تاجر السلاح)

٣ :

جلسة

(يدخل بولونيوس ويضع ملفات على مكاتب كلاوديوس و جيرترود)

(يدخل أعضاء المؤتمر)

(جرس لبدء الجلسة)

بولونيوس: ولاء وزير لمليكه وبلده يتعدّى الحدود العقلانية للواجب. حب يتحدى العوالم الطبيعية للوظيفة البشرية، حب يمكن ـ حالتي هذه، يا مولاي، أن يقارن بولاء الجندي الأخير، البطل الذي تخوض ركبتيه ـ دم زملائه، محاطا بآلاف الأعداء والدبابات وطائرات الهليوكوبتر، وكتائب المشاة ومدافع الهاون، يتفاخر بعلمه بالموت الوشيك، يطلق الطلقات الأخيرة من بندقيته الروسية القديمة و يقع، يا مولاي، يقع مصابا برصاصة ـ القلب الذي يواصل الخفقان لمدة ساعتين أخرتين على الأقل! حب غير عقلاني! تضحية مطلقة ! استسلام كامل لإرادة الملك والدولة – هذا ما أقدمه.

جيرترود: هل يتعين على إفطاري أن يعاني من تضحية هذا الرجل ؟

بولونيوس: إفطاري هو إفطارك سيدتي.

كلاوديوس: بولونيوس! افصح.

بولونيوس: (يعدّل جلسته) لو تمكنت من تفسير هذا الأمر لنفسي، لتمكنت من التعبير عن نفسي، إلا إن هذا الأمر خارج ......إن ابنك مجنون، سيدتي، مجنون! انه ينجرف أكثر وأكثر إلى دوائر التطرف في فكره وسلوكه وأقول لك انه مجنون !

كلاوديوس: سيفتتح البرلمان خلال أقل من ساعة.

بولونيوس: مسألة دقائق مولاي أرجوك ؛ أوفيليا!

أوفيليا (تقرأ قصيدة هاملت) :

اللاجئ الذي يقف على الأسلاك المعدنية لقلبك،

لا رصيد في اسمه،

لا إيداعات،

ولا أسلحة،

منبوذ ومنفي :

أتدمي أغانيه روحك خلف الحدود ؟

بولونيوس : لاحظ النزعة الجنونية في هذه الأغنية القصيرة الكريهة. لاحظ الارتياب في رأس السّلطة. هيا اوفيليا!

أوفيليا: عندما ينهار العالم

وتسقط السموات

(يدخل هاملت)

وتلتهم النيران الفضاء

وتقترب الفردوس من الأرض

في ذلك اليوم،

اعلمي إنني أبحث عنك.

(يخرج هاملت)

بولونيوس :لاحظ ملامح التخريب، لاحظ التعطّش للتغيير العنيف و الشامل للنظام العالمي. لدي دراسات سوف تفسر حلقات الربط بين هذا النوع من الخيال والأعمال الإرهابية.

جيرتروود :هذه الأشعار هي أعمال مراهقين، بولونيوس، ولا تثبت شيئًا.

بولونيوس :كلا، مولاتي، انظري ماذا وجدت بين أوراقه! (**يعرض منشورات جبهة النضال الشعبية**) ليست واحدة ولا عشرة بل الآلاف منها يا مولاي الآلاف!!

كلاوديوس :هذا أمر خطير !

أوفيليا :إن الحزن يمكن أن يدفع -

جيرتروود :الحزن، نعم ! الحزن !

أوفيليا :الجنون !

جيرترود :نعم!

أوفيليا :الجنون !

كلاوديوس :يجب تأخير الزفاف .

أوفيليا :أي زفاف ؟ !

جيرترود :إلى أن نلمس دليلا اضافيا على مدى خطورة التغير المدعى والذي لحق بولدي بسبب حزنه.

كلاوديوس : دليلا إضافيا إذاً، بولونيوس ؟

أوفيليا : أي زفاف ؟ !

بولونيوس : ابنتي ستقدم الدليل.

أوفيليا : أي زفاف ؟ !!!

جيرتروود : حقا ؟ وكيف ؟

بولونيوس : أوفيليا؟

أوفيليا : نعم؟

بولونيوس : في المرة القادمة التي ترين فيها هاملت، سوف تسألينه – بطريقة غير مباشرة ومعسولة طبعاً – أسئلة مثل " أين كنت؟... ماذا كنت تكتب؟... ماذا تفعل بلياليك؟"

أوفيليا : بإمكاني أن افعل ذلك؟

جيرتروود : ستجيدين الكذب بشكل ممتاز.

أوفيليا : لن أصل إلى مهارتك، سيدتي .

جيرتروود : عفوا - ماذا قلت ؟

كلاوديوس : جميعنا ولدنا كذابين سيئين، سوف تتعلمين يا ابنتي. اسأليه "هل تؤم المساجد" ؟

بولونيوس : " من هم أصدقاؤك؟... وما هي أسماؤهم ؟"

كلاوديوس : " ماذا تقرأ ؟"

جيرتروود : يجب على أحدهم أن يكون معها، بإمكانها أن تكذب.

بولونيوس : سنكون معها سيدتي، اتركي هذا الأمر لي (بنبرة رسمية) سوف

يؤجل الزفاف الملكي، بانتظار اثبات ميول الأمير هاملت التخريبية.

(يتم التصويت وتخرج اوفيليا بانفعال شديد)

بولونيوس : بالاجماع!

كلاوديوس : "يمكرون و يمكر الله و الله خير الماكرين".

بولونيوس : صدق الله العظيم.

(جرس نهاية الجلسة.)

4 :

هاملت، وحيدا في الصحراء، وتسمع عن بعد أصوات الفرقة العسكرية وتعلن مكبرات الصوت عن افتتاح البرلمان الجديد.

هاملت : لقد خلت القرى التي كانت في قلبي،

وحجارة الأرصفة تعصف بها الريح.

أرواح الرجال من الرابعة عشرة و حتى الأربعين

أخذوا جميعهم إلى الواجهة البحرية

وغمرت رؤوسهم في المياه الضحلة.

عندما يعبر الظهر الميدان كأرملة

أنا الجرس الشبح الذي يتأرجح في الكنائس،

أنا المنارة التي يمتد لسانها في الرمال،

أنا الطفل الذي في يده رصاصة يبكي بين الصخور،

أنا البغل الذي يتأمل القرد،

بينما تسطر الرياح عاري على البحار.

(يدخل تاجر السلاح)

تاجر السلاح : أنت لست في حفل الافتتاح.

هاملت : لقد فقد الاحتفال سحره.

تاجر السلاح : نحن متشابهان، نفضل البقاء في الظل.

هاملت : هل تتعقبني؟

تاجر السلاح : ربما.

هاملت : كيف الفندق؟

تاجر السلاح : لدي جناح الآن.

هاملت : مبروك.

تاجر السلاح : هناك كلام كثير يدور حولك: البعض يعتقد انك ما تزال في أوروبا، وآخرون يظنون أنك تخطط للهرب، لكن لا أحد يعرف تماما ما الذي تنوي فعله، أليس كذلك؟

هاملت : (يسرح نظره في الأفق) في صغري كان الأفق أكثر ألوانا وأكثر بهاء، أكثر رحابة.

تاجر السلاح : خطر على بالي أن نكون أصدقاء يوما. فأنت في حاجة إلى إنسان تثق به، وأنا أعرف ما معنى العزلة. أمامك مستقبل عظيم، ونتمنى أن تنشأ بيننا علاقة لتعزيز تطلعاتك.

هاملت : ما الذي تعرفه عن الفوسفور؟

تاجر السلاح : الفسفور؟ يكون انتفاخات صغيرة بيضاء، كنار الشواء.

هاملت : ألا يحرق؟

تاجر السلاح: ألم تسمع بقصة الطفل وحفّار القبور؟

هاملت : قصها علي.

تاجر السلاح: عندما رفع منع التجول، كان الطفل قد توفي منذ خمسة أيام، فأحضروا حفّار القبور. أعد له قبرا عميقا وضيقا، وبعد إقامة الصلوات عليه، جرف عليه أول كومة من التراب : فانفجرت الجثة الصغيرة بألسنة من اللهب وأصيب حفّار القبور بالعمى: هذا هو الفوسفور.

هاملت: هل تستطيع أن تزودني البعض منه ؟

تاجر السلاح: أستطيع .

هاملت: جيد.

تاجر السلاح: على الأمير أن يتشبث بعلوم الجن والإنس. لو كان البشر كلهم أفاضل لأصبح هذا بلا معنى، لكن ...

(يقع انفجار عن بعد، تتوقف الفرقة العسكرية عن العزف وتستبدل بالصفارات.)

هاملت: ما هذا ؟

تاجر السلاح: ليست لدي أدنى فكرة .

(يخرجان معاً)

٥ :

جلـــــسة

(يدخل كلاوديوس وبولونيوس)

مؤتمر هاملت

كلاوديوس: أعثر عليهم !

بولونيوس: لم يعلن أحدا مسئوليته، لا مؤشرات، لا اتصالات، لا شيء.

كلاوديوس: إن خطوط أنابيب البترول مهددة، والمستثمرون مرعوبون !

بولونيوس: لدي ٢٠ عنصرا من جبهة النضال الشعبية تحت التعذيب، و رؤوس التنظيمات الدينية تمت محاصرتهم. لدي عشرون وحدة استخباراتية في شبكة تلتف حول المدينة، والرجال يطهرون البالوعات، أيا كانوا، لن يفلتوا من قبضتي.

كلاوديوس: أريد أن أرى وجوه مفجّري السيارات على صفحات الجرائد غدا. وإلا فسوف أكتب استقالتك عنك .

بولونيوس: لقد استدعيت لايارتيس كي يوجز لنا التطورات في الجنوب.

(يدخل لايارتيس)

كلاوديوس: ما أخبارك، لايارتيس؟

لايارتيس: مولاي، إن مؤشرات الحرب تتجمع بسرعة . حتى هذا الصباح تمركز ثلاثة آلاف من رجال فورتنبراس على بعد عشرين كيلو متر من حدودنا الجنوبية. إن الأمور هادئة منذ يومين. لكن وقبل الفجر بساعتين ظهر في الأفق ما ألقى الرعب في قلوب وأرواح رجالنا و جعل عائلات المدنيين تركض في قوافل إلى سياراتهم. من فوق التلال جاء الطاغوت، عامود طوله ١٥ كم من الدبابات البريطانية – ثلاث دبابات جنبا إلى جنب ، تتحرك بسرعة ١٥ كيلو متر في الساعة باتجاه حدودنا.وكأن جيش فورتنبراس بأكمله يتقدم نحونا كأم أربعة وأربعين عملاقة مدرّعة. لقد كانت وكأنها تمزق السطح الاسفلتي في الطريق السريع. و الآن أصبح الطريق الساحلي والبحر مغطيين بالدبابات والمدفعية الثقيلة على طول ٢٠ كيلو متر.

كلاوديوس: نحن معتادون على هذه التكتيكات، يا لايارتيس، ولا أرى أي داع للهلع.

(يدخل هاملت حاملاً قطعة من مركبة تم تفجيرها متظاهرا بالصمم بسبب الانفجار.)

بولونيوس: أين كنت ؟

هاملت : آسف على التأخير، هل رأيت الازدحام ؟

لايارتيس : (الى كلاوديوس) لا داع للهلع، مولاي!؟

بولونيوس : (إلى هاملت) لم تكن في مجلس الأمة.

هاملت: ماذا ؟

كلاوديوس : أبدا.

بولونيوس : مجلس الأمة!

هاملت: أمة؟ أمي؟ أماه؟

بولونيوس : أين كنت ؟

هاملت: لقد انتهيت من لوم أمي. أبلغوا عمي!. انتهيت!. هناك احتفال في الخارج : مئــات، ألــــوف، كلهـم مرششون بالدم، مفعمون ببهجة وطنية، يصرخون في الشوارع. مبارك، مبارك، زعيمنا : روعة!

كلاوديوس : هاملت، لقد حدث هجوم إرهابي أثناء الافتتاح.

هاملت: (مستعرضا قطعة المركبة المنفجرة) ها نحن ذا. انظروا، آووه انظروا !

كلاوديوس : هجوم إرهابي!

هاملت: آبي؟أحبابي! أنتم أحبابي! لقد وجدت هذا !

بولونيوس : لقد جنّ.

هاملت: إنها نصب تذكاري. سوف أعطيها لأوفيليا كرمز لقلبي الدامي! لا، ان

ذلك محزن جدا. سوف أعطيها لعمي! نعم عمي أعطني قبلة وسوف أعطيك هذا النصب التذكاري.

كلاوديوس: سوف نتركه، هيا لايارتيس.

هاملت : أوه هيا، عمي، إن قبلاتك ليست بمثل قبلات أوفيليا! أرجوك خذه، عمي اعطه لأمي كرمز لحبك العاثر لها، لسوف تحبه! عمي إن إرادة الأمة بين ذراعي أرجوك خذها مني.

بولونيوس: مولاي، سنتركك الآن.

هاملت: (وحده) عمي! عمي؟؟

(تطفأ الأنوار).

الفصل الثالث - العصر

١ :

اللوحـــة الأولى

الوقت: ٧ : ٤٥ صباحا

بولونيوس : كل شيء على ما يرام ؟

تاجر السلاح : افتتاح البرلمان هزنا في أعماقنا.

بولونيوس : (يقرأ من تصريح صحفي) هؤلاء الأعداء المتغطرسون أقزام . هم يبصقون على العملاق لكن العملاق يبصق عليهم ويسحقهم. إنهم خونة، مرتزقة، قراصنة.

تاجر السلاح : نحن نسميهم إرهابيين (Terrorists).

بولونيوس : يا الله أحب هذه المفردة! أيمكنك أن تكتبها لي ؟

تاجر السلاح : بسرور (يأخذ منه القلم)

بولونيوس : (وهو يحاول أن يقرأ) Te - rro-ri

تاجر السلاح : Terrorists

بولونيوس : Tero-ri

تاجر السلاح : Terrorists

بولونيوس : Terror-ro

تاجر السلاح : Terrorists

بولونيوس : Terrorists يا ! يا للعبارة الرائعة محشوة بالمال.

تاجر السلاح :   نعم بخصوص المال

بولونيوس : ما في مشكلة. ما في مشكلة، حبيبي.

تاجر السلاح : متى؟

بولونيوس : متى؟ متى؟ يأتي البعير.

تاجر السلاح : عند توقيع العقد.

بولونيوس : بالكامل؟

تاجر السلاح : بالكامل !

(يخرج تاجر السلاح ومعه قلم بولونيوس)

بولونيوس : قلمي! .... Terrorist !

٢-١

الوقت : ١٠ : ١٥ صباحا

هاملت : من هو كلاوديوس؟

لايارتيس : لم تستوعب. أليس كذلك؟

هاملت : من هو ؟

لايارتيس : انه قائدنا وسيدنا الأكبر .

هاملت : وزعيمنا و مهيبنا و طويل أعمارنا و طويل أنوفنا- ألا زلت في القبيلة لايارتيس؟

لايارتيس : و ماذا تريد؟العامل لا يجد مصنعاً يعمل فيه المفكر متقطع الأنفاس مشتت الجذور-

هاملت : كما أنتم: يولى عليكم.

لايارتيس : الشعب بحاجة إلى اله !

هاملت : أعلم الآن أين تقف أنت!

لايارتيس : إن فرض الانقسام والانشقاق الداخلي هو انتحار سياسي. وهو استراتيجية طفل غاضب.

هاملت: انه قاتل.

لايارتيس : كذلك جميع القادة.

هاملت: (يهمس) لقد قتل أبي.

لايارتيس : فورتنبراس هو من كتب ذلك السطر. انه هراء وأنت تعلم ذلك.

هاملت: سأثبت لك ذلك.

لايارتيس: حسنا، أعلمني.

هاملت: أريدك هنا معي، لايارتيس، المعركة الحقيقية هنا.

لايارتيس : أعلمني عندما تنتهي.

هاملت: من ماذا؟

لايارتيس : من تبرير عبثك.

(تطفأ الأنوار).

٣-١

الوقت: ١:٣٠ ظهراً

جيرترود : أين كان ذلك، باريس؟

تاجر السلاح: زيوريخ.

جيرترووود: طبعا زيوريخ! وكيف حال كلابك ؟

تاجر السلاح: لقد استثمرت للتو في كلب صيني أصيل.

جيرترووود: آه ! لدي كلبة مكسيكية صلعاء و أصيلة، يجب أن نعرفهما على بعض!

تاجر السلاح: سننجب وحشا مخيفا.

جيرترود: كم أنت ودود.

تاجر السلاح: وأنت أصيلة النسب.

جيرترووود: أشكرك. لا أريد أن أزعجك معي، لكن لدي مزرعة في الجنوب، مزرعتي الخاصة، واعتقد إنها بحاجة إلى ترميم امني و كنت اتساءل إذا كان بوسعك–

تاجر السلاح: أنا أعشق الريف، وأظن أنني أعرف مزرعتك.

جيرترووود: حقا؟

تاجر السلاح: أهذه هي؟ (يريها بعض الصور) كم تبدين رائعة كما خلقك ربك.

جيرترود: سأحتفظ بهذه الصور.

تاجر السلاح: اعذريني، انها مجرد نسخ.

جيرترووود: كما قلت لك – الموقع في حاجة إلى المزيد من الأمن.

تاجر السلاح: بكل سرور وإلى أين نتجه ؟

جيرترووود: إلى البحر.

تاجر السلاح: أشمه من هنا.

(يخرجان معاً).

١-٤

الوقت: ١:٣١ ظهراً

هاملت: إن الأعداء على الحدود وهم يغذونه فيكم، ويريدون منكم تصديقه: وهم!

لايارتيس: الناس يموتون في كل يوم، أنا أراهم، أرى القنابل التي تقتلهم، وأرى الجنود الذين يطلقون النار عليهم، أسمع السياسيين الذين يوجهونهم، انه ليس وهما.

هاملت: إن العدو الحقيقي هنا، في القصر، بيننا.

لايارتيس: لن يكون هناك من أحد نقاتل من أجله إلا إذا هزمنا فورتبراس.

هاملت: لن يكون هناك من شعب نفقده إلا إذا تخلصنا من العفن الذي يلتهمنا من الداخل.

لايارتيس: هاملت، فليكن الله في عونك. سأترك لك هذا

(يضع مسدسا على الطاولة ويخرج)

هاملت: لايارتيس... أخي.

(تطفأ الأنوار).

٢ :

جيرتروود بصحبة أوفيليا. وهي تهديها مجوهرات.

أوفيليا : ممن هذه ؟

جيرترووود : من هاملت! والآن، أرجوك لا تتحدثي بالسياسة وإياك أن تتلفظي بكلمة واحدة عن الدين. ليكن حديثك كله عن الحب وذلك من دون مباشرة. فابني مرهف الإحساس لايطيق لحظة الخطاب المباشر اسأليه عن قصائده وعززي السؤال بطلب المزيد منها تجنبي السخافات، تعرفين حدة ذكائه إبقيه مشدود الانتباه، جددي له طمأنتك بإشارة أو بدمعة .لا، لاتبكي، سيعتقد أن هناك خطأ ما.

(في هذه الأثناء يتوجه هاملت إلى مكتب لايارتيس ليأخذ المسدس)

جيرترووود: وعندما تتزوجان سوف تتذكرين هذا الأمر وتضحكين عاليا منه.

أوفيليا : سوف نفعل، سوف نضحك، سنموت من الضحك.

(هاملت حاملا مسدسا)

هاملت : أ نه لا يزن كثيرا، و لمَ يجب ذلك ؟

إنه يؤدي الغرض، عليه رقم تسلسلي،

فوهته وزناده قد تطورت عبر القرون،

وأسراره تم تناقلها من الأب للإبن، انها آلة رائعة.

انها لي ألمعها بقطن مصري ،

بينما انا مريض باحلام اليقظة

أغذي عبثي من باب الى باب

أدور وأدور حول متجر الأحزان.

لا حماسة شهيد تؤجج هذا الجسد

لا أحلام بالجنة، لا شوق للعدالة، لا توق للتغيير

أمعائي كأمعاء الخنزير :

لا ترفض أي قذارة!

كرهي كحبي ناقص لا كمال فيه،

لاشيء بطولياً، لا شيء منفّراً،

مجرد ردائة تافهة، يحتملها عبثي،

طوبى لهذا المال

يطفأ ببرود الجلّاد وبصبر القنّاص

النيران في صدري

النار التي ألهبت روحي

من الآن وحتى مماتي

(يقـرأ الرقـم التسلسلي علـى المسـدس) ٥٥٢٤٧٩٤ (يتصـارع مـع رغبة بالانتحار)

إن السقم في داخلي أقوى مني

والنفس كالكلبة تعوي على بوابة المسلخ !

(دخول كلاوديوس وبولونيوس مرتديان عباءتان سوداوان، تعدل جيرترود العباءتان وتخرج)

كلاوديوس : شكرا جيرترود.

(بولونيوس وكلاوديوس يحثان أوفيليا على الحوار مع هاملت)

أوفيليا : هاملت ،أنا أدعو الله أن يحميك هاملت.

هاملت : أوفيليا! أنا مصغٍ إليك!

أوفيليا : أشكرك على هداياك.

هاملت : أي هدايا؟

أوفيليا : لا يهم.

هاملت : لا أدري إن كنت يوما قلت لك .....

أوفيليا : لا تفعل ....

هاملت : دعيني،لا تقاطعيني! لدي حاجة رهيبة لتغيير نفسي، أو بالأحرى، بالأحرى، هناك تغييرات....

أوفيليا : لا تخبرني الآن.

هاملت : وإذا لم أخبرك الآن ...

أوفيليا : إذاً أخبرني الآن هيا تحدث !

هاملت : أوفيليا؟

أوفيليا : نعم.

هاملت : أي هدايا ؟ أي هدايا ؟ (**وقفة طويلة**) هل حانت الساعة ؟

أوفيليا : ماذا ؟

هاملت : الساعة التي ستأخذك مني ؟

أوفيليا : كلا.

هاملت : هل سأرغم على كرهك الآن ؟

أوفيليا : كلا! إنها بعيدة، بعيدة جدا.

هاملت : لكن الساعة قد حانت.

أوفيليا : أنا مازلت هنا.

هاملت: لقد ابتعدت.

أوفيليا : أنت تحبني.

هاملت: كلا، كلا: أنا لا ألومك، لكن، لكن، لكن

أوفيليا : حاول أن تحبني........

هاملت: ولا أستطيع مسامحتك، أنت تفهمين؟

أوفيليا : لا تفعل هذا.

هاملت : كيف أستطيع أن أحبك ؟

أوفيليا : حاول ....

هاملت : سوف أطهّر هذه الأرض، سأجعلها نقية، أنا أفهم، أنا فعلا أفهم، لكني سوف أطهرها من أجلك، سوف أعدّها لعودتك، ولو كلفني ذلك حياتي، سوف أنظفها، سوف أطهرها، ستفيض الدماء، سأجعلها تفيض سيولا، أقسم برحمة أبي، وأقسم بالله ولكنك ستعودين، أوفيليا ستعودين. (يخرج)

أوفيليا : (تغني)   مولاي، الى اين؟

خذني لسوق مدينتنا الواسع

بعني بالذهب اللامع

لتطلي بوابة قصرك ذاك

ارحمني مولاي

وخذني، هناك..

(تخرج أوفيليا)

٣ :

جلســـة

(جرس بداية الجلسة)

جيـرتروود : إنها تفسـد عقل ابنـي. أريد إرسالها إلى المحمية.

بولونيـوس : أي محمية، سيدتي؟

جيـرتروود : المحمية الوطنية، محمية القائد في الجنوب لحماية الحيوانات من امثالها. يجب أن تذهب.

بولونيـوس : إن سيدتي غاضبة ومتأثرة بالبشاعة التي حصلت، ولا تستطيع أن تتخذ قرارا حكيما الآن.

كلاوديـوس: جيرتروود، نحن نرفض التهور.

جيـرتروود : و أنا أصرّ.

كلاوديـوس: بولونيوس، فلتجد لنفسها ملجأ خارج المدينة لبضعة أيام. لن يكون هناك حديث عن زواج بعد الآن. انه يسبب لابننا مزاجا سيئا. ولكن الاستثمارات أمرٌ حيوي للاقتصاد في هذه المرحلة من الإعداد للحرب، ومزاج ابننا يبدو انطوائيا ولا يخدم المصلحة العامة. إن الأمن القومي يتطلب أن يرسل هاملت أيضا بعيدا. الى أين سيدتي؟

(وقفة)

جيـرتروود : بيروت؟

بولونيـوس : فيها العديد من المليشيات.

جيـرتروود : دمشـق؟

كلاوديـوس: العديد من البعثيين؟

بولونيوس : القاهرة ؟

جيرتروود : الكثير من العبثيين.

بولونيوس : صنعاء ؟

جيرتروود : الكثير من المتمردين.

كلاوديوس: الرباط ؟

جيرتروود : الكثير من الحشاشين.

كلاوديوس: السودان ؟

بولونيوس : الكثير من السود.

جيرتروود : جدّة ؟

كلاوديوس: الكثير من العصي.

جيرتروود : طهران ؟

كلاوديوس: الكثير من العمائم.

بولونيوس : باريس ؟

كلاوديوس: الكثير من النساء.

جيرتروود: واشنطن ؟

بولونيوس : لن يتمكن من دخولها !

كلاوديوس: لندن ؟

بولونيوس و جيرتروود : لندن !!

كلاوديوس: ضعه على أول طائرة إلى لندن، وأبلغ وزير الخارجية بأنه قادم

للمقامرة في بيكاديللي، وقدم له دفتر شيكات حكومياً.

بولونيوس: لكن مولاي، قصفت دبابات فورتنبراس المطار هذا الصباح ....

كلاوديـوس : أغلق الطريق السريع، فبإمكانه استخدامه للإقلاع.

(تصويت)

بولونيوس : بالإجماع.

جيـرتـروود : لن يذهب ابني دون مراسيم حفل وداع!

بولونيـوس : فعلاً..ولابد للصحافة أن تنقل ذلك.

كلاوديوس : حفل وداع رسمي إذاً.

(تمر النفاثات فوق الرؤوس و تهتز الطاولات من شدة الانفجار)

كلاوديوس : إن المستقبل مشرق . وأنا أشكركم.

(يهمّون بالخروج. وفيما هم متجمعون في الممر)

هاملت: فلتنصبّ لعنـــات الجحيم على أمك وأم أمـك وأم أم أمــك. لا تجـاوبنــي! لا تحملق بوجهي يا قائد بالوكالة! يا عميل! هل تعرف ابن من أنا !! ان مجرّد ذكر اسمـه يجعلك ترتجف !!

(يخرج كلاوديوس)

هاملت : رجل تافه (مخاطبا الموسيقيين) هيا أنتما. اعزفا لي مقاما قديما. نقيا روحي أعزفا .

(تعزف الموسيقى).

٤ :

أوفيليا : هل أنت الشيطان ؟

تاجر السلاح: وهل أعجبتك؟

أوفيليا : و لو افترضنا ؟

تاجر السلاح: هل عرفت رجلاً من قبل؟ اسبق وكنت وحيدة في العتمة بجوار ذكر فحل ؟

أوفيليا : (صمت)

تاجر السلاح : إنك ترتجفين. اقتربي مني.

أوفيليا : قرب وجهك مني، وأغمض عينيك. (**تستل سكينا**)

تاجر السلاح: (**يلوي يدها ويرميها على الأرض، فتصرخ من الألم**) ما أروع الصرخة الرقيقة. يا ملائكة الليل خبئوا وجوهكم، لقد أوقع الشيطان بواحدة منكم في أسره. أنا ألبي كل الرغبات، فما رغبتك يا أوفيليا ؟

أوفيليا : أريد قبلة.

تاجر السلاح: قبلة ؟

أوفيليا : قبلة.

تاجر السلاح: قبلة!

أوفيليا : قبلة.

تاجر السلاح: قبلة.

أوفيليا : قبلة.

تاجر السلاح: قبلة .

أوفيليا : قبلة.

تاجر السلاح : كبيرة أم صغيرة؟

أوفيليا : لا يهم

(تطفأ الأنوار)

٥ :

(يدخل هاملت من بين طاولات المجلس إلى المنتصف وهي المنطقة المحرمة أي فضاء على الخشبة لم يتم استعماله حتى الآن)

هاملت : هذا الفضاء التام... ما الذي أوجده ؟ هذه هي الهوة التي تبتلع ألفاظنا وتأسر كلماتنا وعند هذا الخط ترتجف أقدامنا ونشيح بناظرينا عن هذا الربع الخالي الذي يستحيل خرقه! هنا سوف أحفر وأرقص! هنا سأمسك بجذور هذا القصر وأنبش نتف الحقيقة من بين أكداس جثث الموتى. سأخرج تلك الجثث وأحييها، أريدها أن تصرخ عبر الممرات، أن تركض عارية عبر الحدائق، وعندئذ من يجرؤ على القول أن هاملت قد رأى وبات كالصنم ؟

(تطفأ الآنوار)

(تدخل جيرتروود وبولونيوس)

جيرتروود : هنا ؟

بولونيوس : أجل.

جيرتروود : هل أنت متأكد، بولونيوس؟

بولونيوس : كان مصمما يا سيدتي، بل رسم لي خريطة.

جيرتروود : أرني إياها.

(يدخل كلاوديوس)

كلاوديوس : مستحيل!

جيرتروود : كلاوديوس، هذه ليلته الأخيرة.

كلاوديوس : ابحثي عن مكان آخر.

جيرتروود : لا تضخم الأمر!

كلاوديوس : لم أقف هنا أبدا، ولا أحد غيري تجرأ على ذلك، ولا ارى سببا للوقوف هنا لمجاملة ابنك المعتوه.

جيرتروود : كلاوديوس، أرجوك!

كلاوديوس : بولونيوس، اخرج حالا!!

(يدخل تاجر السلاح)

تاجر السلاح: مساء الخير بفخاماتكم .

جيرتروود : مرحبا بك، يا للمفاجأة!

كلاوديوس : كنا في انتظارك!

تاجر السلاح : أخبرني هاملت أنكم تقيمون حفلا صغيرا.

كلاوديوس : يسعدني انك استطعت الحضور.

تاجر السلاح : تبدين رائعة، سيدتي!

جيرتروود : شكرا (**تدخل أوفيليا**) يا إلهي! أوفيليا: تبدين كالأموات

بولونيوس : كانت في الخارج والطقس بارد قليلا .

أوفيليا : كنت أتقيأ طوال اليوم.

تاجر السلاح : مسكينة ! هل أنت محمومة؟

أوفيليا : لا تلمسني!

كلاوديوس : هه!

جيرتروود : تعكر مزاجها لأن هاملت مسافر!

بولونيوس : بالعكس، بل هي منزعجة كونها ستغادر قريبا.

تاجر السلاح : كنت اريد اعانتها، لا أكثر.

بولونيوس : شكراً

كلاوديوس : هل أحضرت التلفزيون؟

بولونيوس : أنهم يصورون فيما نحن نتحدث، بث غير مباشر طبعا.

كلاوديوس : وما هو برنامج الحفل؟

بولونيوس : سنتصافح ونتعانق، ثم نتناول بعض العصير و المعجنات ومن ثم رأسا إلى الطائرة.

كلاوديوس : إني أتعرق.

بولونيوس : عفوا (يمسح جبين كلاوديوس)

(يدخل هاملت على حصان من عجينة الورق وهو يرتدي ثياب الفارس العربي القديم).

هاملت : مساء الخير يا قوم!! قوم لوط!

جيرتروود : هاملت، ما هذا الهذر؟

هاملت : هذر ؟ أنا أستعد للحرب، سيدتي، ألم تسمعي ان العدو على الأبواب؟ اسأليه! الليلة نكرم كبارنا، ونحي الحصان، حصان الحرب.

بولونيوس : ولماذا عينا فرسك مغمضتان ، يا مولاي ؟

هاملت: لحمايتهما من النظرات الحاسدة، ومن ابتسامة أوفيليا السامة!

تاجر السلاح: هل حصانك جائع يا سيدي؟

هاملت: طبعا! هو شديد الجوع دائما! لأنه فرس مطر اد! يبتلع دوما!! (تاجر الأسلحة يقدم مكعبات السكر) آه! مكعبات السكر، يا لك من فارس رائع! إذاً فلنطعم حصان الحرب. عماه، كما ﴾ كل الأمور، يجب أن تكون أنت البادئ أنت الملك! (بينما **يطعم كلاوديوس حصان الحرب بمكعبات من السكر يخرج هاملت سكيناً لعبة ويطعن فيها كلاوديوس)** أوه ،آه، قد، حصاني يحتضر! عماه، لقد قتلته. ليت أمي تحسن البكاء، فإنه قد ينهض ثانية! أمي!! هل جفت دموعك تماما ؟ غارت؟ (تقترب جيرترود إلى إبنها فيعض هاملت أذنها بشراسة) لكن انظروا، ها هو ينهض، لا بد أن فيك بعض البلل و شيء من البلاء. آوه ها هو حصاني قد قام، لم يستطع عمي أن يميته. طبعا هو غير قادر على أن يميته، هناك عسر هضم فقط، هذا كل ما ﴾ الأمر حصان الحرب! امضغ المزيد ! أمي، طبطبي عليه، لكن اياك ان تقبله، أماه. فهو حصان شبق جدا ! أوفيليا، تبدين حبلى، أأرسلتها الى الجبهة يا عماه ؟ (تخرج أوفيليا) عليك أن ترسلها للجبهة عماه، لكي تخدم الوطن و ترفع من معنويات تلك الآلاف من الحشود.   (يخاطب تاجر السلاح)   أما أنت، فكلك سكر ويكفي أن يلحس الحصان يدك. والآن، رفعت الأقلام وجفت الصحف! فلننشد: **(يغني)** "أرواحنا الثمن و المجد للوطن" الى الحرب ! إلى الحرب، أشكركم جميعا. إلى الحرب! (هاملت يخرج)

كلاوديوس: سنرسله إلى لندن لإجراء الفحوص عليه.

تاجر السلاح: أعرف بعض المتخصصين.

جريرترود: حقا؟ أيمكنك أن تعطيني أسماءهم ؟

تاجر السلاح: بكل سرور !

بولونيوس: وكيف سنظهر ما حدث هنا للرعية، يا سيدي ؟

كلاوديوس: كما حدث.As is!

مؤتمر هاملت

(تصدر أصوات غريبة عبر مكبرات الصوت)

جيرتروود : ما ذلك الصوت المخيف ؟

كلاوديوس : ماذا يجري، بولونيوس ؟

بولونيوس : تشابك بسيط في جهاز الإنتركم، لا تقلق.

هاملت : (عبر مكبرات الصوت) انتظروا، انتظروا.

كلاوديوس : (إلى بولونيوس) تصرف!

تاجر السلاح : ربما انه يحمل سلاح.

كلاوديوس : بولونيوس! يا وغد!

هاملت : انتظروا، انتظروا.

كلاوديوس : هذا غير مقبول.

(يسمع صوت هاملت عبر مكبرات الصوت : "عمي")

جيرتروود : هاملت، توقف فورا.

كلاوديوس : بولونيوس، أعطني مسدسك.

(ترفع الستارة فتظهر صورة في منتهى السخرية والتهكم وكأنما هي من أعمال الفنان ناجي العلي حيث نرى جيرتروود وهي متمددة على ظهرها بينما يستلقي عليها كلاوديوس وكلاوديوس يستلقي عليه تاجر السلاح وجميعهم قد استلقوا على هاملت الأب طاعنين جثة هذا الأخير بسكاكين عديدة)

بولونيوس : حرس ! حرس ! حرس!

(أضواء.)

٦ :

كلاوديـوس : انه خطر! أريد تصفيته.

جيرتروود : سأتحدث إليه.

كلاوديـوس : بولونيـوس !

بولونيـوس : مولاي !

جيرتروود : قلت سأتحدث إليه.

كلاوديـوس : أعط الأمـر.

جيرتروود : إغرائي، كلاوديوس! إن إغرائي يروّض حلفاءك، ويقوّض أعداءك، يرضي الشعب كله ويكفل شيكاتك. لاشيء يحدث من دوني، الا تفهم؟ لاشيء! انا سوف أتحدث إلى ولدي.

كلاوديـوس : قبل نهاية اليوم.

بولونيـوس : سأرافق سيدتي، يجب أن نتوقع الأسوأ.

كلاوديـوس : أشكرك، يا زوجتي **(تخرج جيرترروود)** لقد أفرغت البنـك المركـزي، بولونيـوس،سترانـي لاحقـا لتلبيـة حاجتك.

بولونيـوس : مولاي، إن القادة بانتظار قرارك.

كلاوديـوس : فلينتظروا!

(يخرج بولونيوس)

مؤتمر هاملت

7:

كلاوديوس : (يفتح شنطة صغيرة) دولارات البترول. آه يا ربّي، يا رب المال، علمني معنى دولارات البترول. لا رب لي إلا أنت، خلقت على صورتك، التمس الهداية منك يا من ترى كل شيء وتسمع كل شيء رب العالمين، والرخاء والقانون. **(يخرج رزماً من الدولارات ويوزعها على الطاولة)** ... هذا للفضائية وهذا لأقمارك يا ربي... وهذا للفيلم عن حياتي البطولية، وهذا لشركات الإنتاج الرّبانية، وهذا لكاميرات التجسس عبر العاصمة، وهذا للتقنيين التابعين لك يا رب، هذا للابتدائية والثانوية والجامعة، وهذا للمناهج الرّبانية، وهذا لي. إنهم متخمون بكل عطايا السماء وأنا العربي القذر أضيع و أهدر البلايين لأعبدك، أنا واضح وشفاف، شفاف وصاف كجدول رقراق. أتوسل إليك مولاي، ساعدني، لا تجعلني كريها في نظرك، يا رب. أنا لا اتنافس معك، كيف يمكن لهذه الأكداس من اللحم الآدمي التنافس مع خلودك؟ **(يبدأ كلاوديوس بخلع ثيابه)** أنا وكيلك، ولست شريكا رديئا لشراهتك وبذاءتك اللامتناهية.أنا لا أحاول أن أصبح نقيا طاهرا: لقد تعلمت الكثير من البذاءة والقذارة، انا ملك القذارة وفنّان القذارة، أصنع تلالا من أجساد البشر،وأقدم الأضحيات تمجيدا لك، أنا أعشق رائحة جثث الأقليات المتعفنة، التي عطّرناهم بتقنياتك الغازية، وعلى رغم أي ادعّاء أنت، أنت الّرب . إن وزراءك الملائكيين يريدون التخلص مني، يريدون طردي من حضن رحمتك كإبليس، ولكن من وضعني هنا، آوه يا ربّي دعنا لا ننسى من وضعني هنا ؟ أمامك، أنا مخلوق أعزل، أيمكن أن يكون قبحي لا يطاق الآن؟ أنفي لم يزدد انعقافا عن ذي قبل، وعيناي لم تزدد شيطانية عما كانتا عليه عندما ضيفتنّي عذارى واشنطن وأفيون السي آي ايه. آه، أيمكن أن قبحي يسيء لك الآن يا ربّي؟ لا، لا إن قبحي لا يسيء لك الآن. قنابلك الذريّة، قروضك، وديمقراطية القذارة التي تقطر من شعوبك المنتشية – أريدها جميعا، آه يا ربّي أريد ابتساماتك الصفراء وأريد أجواءك الملتبسة الفاسدة، وأريد بنكك الدولي، أريده أن يضاجعني الآن. يا ربّي!!! فلنكن معا في القذارة،أيمكن ذلك ؟ من دونك لا استطيع احتمال نفسي، لا استطيع، لا استطيع ربّي.

(يدخل هاملت إلى مكتب كلاوديوس حاملاً مسدساً)

هاملـــت: الطريقة الوحيدة لتغيير جغرافيا الصراع هي بوجود جنود مشاة على

الأرض يطلقون الرصاصات في اللحم الآدمي. ها أنذا جندي من المشاة، وهذا هو السرداب الذي يعبق برائحة اللحم المتحلل، إن مشاعري هي مشاعر المحارب الذي يريد وقف الزحف، هنا ينكمش عدوي مرتعدا، وحيدا. ارى قطرات العرق تتلألأ على جلدك، أستطيع ان اشتم خوفك، وان اسمع أنفاسك. اشعر بخوفك الآن، توقف عن التنفس، توقف عن التنفس! أرجوك توقف عن التنفس، أرجوك توقف عن التنفس!

(يعود هاملت إلى مكتبة منهاراً)

الفصل الرابع - المغرب

١ :

(يدخل بولونيوس)

بولونيـوس : مولاي !

كلاوديوس: أبلغ الجنرالات . نحن أصبحنا لوحدنا.

(يخرج كلاوديوس ويجلس بولونيوس على مكتب كلاوديوس)

(تدخل جيرترود)

(جلسة)

جيرتـروود : هاملت، أنت خطر على أمن الدولة.

هاملـت: أمـاه، أنت خطر على أخلاق الدولة.

جيرتـروود : هل هي المخدّرات ؟

هاملـت : هل هو الجنـس ؟

جيرتـروود : تحدث إلي، يا ولد ، هل تتعاون مع المتطرفين؟

هاملـت : بل أنا من يسألك: هل تتعاونين مع الشيطان، سيدتي؟ هل هو بجانبك الآن، يغلفك ؟ هـا! هل يجلس الشيطان بجانبك،جيرتروود ، هل يهمس في أذنك ؟

(يستعد بولونيوس لمغادرة مكتب كلاديوس على عجل، ويعبث أثناء حركته.)

هاملـت : هـا ! هل يحتضنك ويدس يده في صدرك، هل هو هنا ؟ هـا ! هـا ! أم هنا ؟ أم هنـا؟

جيرتـروود : (لبولونيوس) اذهب الآن.

(يطلق هاملت النار باتجاه مكتب كلاوديوس ويردي بولونيوس قتيلاً)

(يتحرك هاملت ليرى الجثة).

جيرترووود : ما هذا !

هاملت : إنا لله وإنا إليه راجعون..اجري أيها الدم، عبر المجاري والقبور، اخرس أفواه المنافقين، واعصف بريحك فوق الأمواج والبحار ... آه، أماه، أماه، مازلت شابا فتيّا، فتيّا جدا على تحمل ثقل السماء. **(يواجه جيرترووود)** إن زوجك قاتل!

جيرترووود : بل أنت القاتل!

هاملت : لقد قتل أبي.

جيرترووود : مات أبوك بسبب خيبته !

هاملت : أنت من أهل الشيطان ! التبسك الشيطان وعدت بلا عقل.

جيرترووود : انظر لنفسك، أأثيرك هاملت؟ أهذا ما في الأمر؟ ألا تستطيع مقاومة جاذبيتي؟ ألهذا الحد أنت مريض!

هاملت : فلتسرع الأرض بدورانها كلما اقترب فجر الحقيقة.

(يصفعها بقوة على وجهها)

جيرترووود : أتجرؤ على صفعي !

هاملت : أجرؤ على أكثر!

جيرترووود : زنديق من أب زنديق !

هاملت : لن يغفر لك الله آثامك!

جيرترووود : (تبصق عليه) عليك وعلى أبيك .

هاملت: لقد تفوقت على بابل الرشيد و سدوم بفجورك !

جيرتروود: ابتعد عني، ابعد يداك عني .

هاملت: إن شريعة الله تبيح لك الزواج من شقيق زوجك فقط عندما لا يكون هناك رجال آخرون أمامك ،ألّا تعلمت يا امرأة؟

جيرتروود: ستسحل في الشوارع على فعلتك، وسأمزق كبدك بأصابع يدي.

هاملت: جيرتروود الجحود !

جيرتروود: سأعلق رأسك على شرفتي.

هاملت : لقد حدث مثل هذا في زمن الرسول، عاهرة انتقلت من ملك إلى بائس ومن قاتل إلى لص، إلى أن وجدت الطريق القويم. هلّا تعلمت يا جيرتروود الجحود! ألا تفكرين بالموت ؟ أأفقدتك الشهوة رشدك ؟

(يغمض عين جيرتروود ويضع المسدس على مكان الرحم)

ابتهلي إلى الله !

ابتهلي إلى الله !

ابتهلي إلى الله !

(عبر مكبرات الصوت. تتلى بصوت جبار الآية الثامنة والعشرون من السورة الخامسة من القرآن الكريم)

".................. "ولا تقل لهما أف ولا تنهرهما"

(يتوقف هاملت برهة و وجهه يعبر عن الخشية و الاضطراب)

جيرتروود: لن تنسى جيرتروود أبدا العار الذي أنزلته بها، وصمة العار هذه لن تزول!.

(تخرج جيرتروود)

هاملت: آه، يا الهي، لقد تماديت! احذروا انتقـام الأم.

قال ثم من قال أمك

قال ثم منْ قال أمك

قال ثم منْ قال أمك

سامحيني أماه سامحيني.

أماه؟

أماه؟

أماه؟

(تطفأ الأنوار)

٢ :

(يدخل كلاوديوس ويكتشف جثة بولونيوس)

كلاوديوس: إرهابي، إرهابي، إرهابي! لن نسمح لإرهابي جبان أن يدفع بالأمـة إلى حافة الهاوية.

هاملت : انظر حولك: الحظر يطبق عليك من كل جانب، قادة العـالم يرفضون اتصالاتك، أموال دولتي تم تجميدهـا !

كلاوديوس: إن إرهابك لن يملي علينـا سياسـتنا : أنت منفي !

هاملت: أوصلنـا إلى هذا الحد ؟

كلاوديوس: نعـم . اذهـب الآن.

هاملت: لو دامت لغيرك ما اتصلت إليك. والى أين يا عمـي ؟

كلاووديوس: لندن !

هاملت: آه، لندن ! لن أكون وحيدا. سآكل القليل، وسأصبح نحيلا، أكتب المنشورات وأصبح الحيوان المدلّل لدى مستنيري أوروبا. جيد، عمي، جيد، أثابك الله. ودمت ذخراً لهذا الوطن. الوداع عمي !

كلاووديوس : لولا الأضواء علينا لقطّعتك إربا إربا. دعها تخفت حينها سأضرب دون أثر.

(يخرج هاملت)

٣ :

كلاووديوس : هل تظنني قرد؟

تاجر السلاح : أبداً، كلاووديوس.

كلاووديوس : خذ هذا (يناوله قائمة)

تاجر السلاح : (يقرأ) خمسمئة مدفع، اثنا عشر ب – ١٢، أربعين حوامه، خمس غواصات، خمسمائة صاروخ كروز، سبعة عشر صاروخ سلك وورم، مليون عبوة من الذخيرة الحربية...أسبوع.

كلاووديوس : لا تتوه لكائن من كان بأنني قرد، وإلا قتلتك، أتفهم ؟

تاجر السلاح : تماما.

كلاووديوس : ششش.

تاجر السلاح : ششش.

(يخرج تاجر السلاح)

٤ :

(هاملت في المقبرة)

هاملت: السلام عليكم ياأهل المقابر،

أيها الموتى، روحي منهكة وغدوت مريضاً،

أنهكت روحي فتن الأحياء،

أقبلت الفتن كقطع الليل المظلم،

يتبع آخرها أولها،

أفيدوني بالله عليكم ياأهل القبور،

كيف تكون الآخرة شراً من الأولى؟ كيف؟ كيف؟

سوف أقضي الأربعين ليلة بينكم،

وسأجعل من عظامكم كتاب معرفتي،

ومن جماجمكم ضوءاً أهتدي به،

بينكم سأمكث صامتاً،

أقتات على أحلام الموتى.

(تطفأ الأنوار)

٥ :

(**كلاوديوس** يتحدث عبرتلفونه الخلوي، بينما تسقط القنابل في الشوارع القريبة).

جيرتروود: كلاوديوس أنا ثملة !

كلاوديوس: أريد مضاعفة الحراسة على حاويات الذخيرة – انسي أمر

توصيل المياه.

جيرتروود: كيف تتركني هنا؟ أنا ثملة !

كلاوديوس: ماذا عن مولّدات الاحتياطي... أعلم هذا! آخر تقدمه قدر استطاعتك مكافأتك عندي يا لواء.

(يدخل لايارتيس)

لايارتيس: إن كلاب الحرب تنبح على دمك كلاوديوس ! اعطني والدي!

كلاوديوس: لقد افتقدتك، لايارتيس.

لايارتيس: أين والدي ؟

كلاوديوس: افتقدت توجيهاتك .

جيرتروود: انه انقلاب !

كلاوديوس: ولاؤك، وقوتك. أكاد اشعر بالقنّاصة يصوبون إلى مؤخرة رأسي — ما الذي حدث لك، لايارتيس؟

لايارتيس: انتظر ردك.

جيرتروود: لايارتيس الصغير يتزعّم انقلابا.

لايارتيس : لن اسمح لأحد بالتلاعب بي! فلتذهب نياشينك الى الجحيم ولتذهب رتبك إلى أقذر الكلاب.

جيرتروود: أنا لست أمك، أنا مليكتك!

لايارتيس: اعطني والدي!

كلاوديوس: إن والدك معي. لقد فقد صوته. وطلب مني أن أسألك لماذا خنته؟

لايارتيس : أنا لم أخنه أبدا.

جيرترود : ارفع صوتك بولونيوس !

كلاوديوس : يسألك هل تركك في حاجة إلى أي شيء؟

جيرترود : ارفع صوتك !

لايارتيس : لِمَ أحتاج إلى أي شيء؟

كلاوديوس : إذاً لم تنحز ميليشياتك إلى فورتبراس ؟ للشياكل؟ للسلاح؟ أم انه الخوف؟ ماذا ينقصك لايارتيس؟

لايارتيس : أرني والدي!

كلاوديوس : إن هاملت يحتجزه كرهينة.

لايارتيس : أين ؟

جيرترود : في قبره.

كلاوديوس : جيرترودا!

لايارتيس : ماذا ؟

جيرترود : ميت !

كلاوديوس : جيرترودا!

(تظهر أوفيليا من خلال بث مسجل)

أوفيليا : هل تسجل ؟ هل أبدأ ؟ بسم الله الرحمن الرحيم

لايارتيس : أوفيليا !

كلاوديوس : لقد جنّت ! يا لايارتيس.

أوفيليا : إن من حوّلني إلى لاجئة صنع مني قنبلة.

حاولت أن أتحدث حديث المرأة

حاولت أن أسامح، وفي ليال كثيرة شحذت لساني

لكن صمتي نزف من بين أسناني

وها أنذا الحيوان المنسي

يتأتئ بلغة البشر

لكن الكذب لا يفيد لا شيء يمكن أن يغير

الظلم في هذه الحياة

اريدكم ان تعلموا بانني سأعبر بجسدي عما تعجزون التعبير عنه

وبذلك الاقي وجه ربي نقية طاهرة روحا وكرامة

أذهب الى ربّي طاهـرة.

ليارتيس : أبي، أترى عيناك هذا؟!

(تطفأ الأنوار)

٩ :

(كلاوديوس ولايارتيس ينقلان جثة بولونيوس.)

كلاوديوس : هاملت يقتل والد لايارتيس، هاملت يفقد شقيقة لايارتيس عقلها. هل خرست أسلحة لايارتيس؟

لايارتيس : ماذا تسألني؟

كلاوديوس : هل نخنق الصحافة؟ هل نلتزم الصمت؟

لايارتيس : بل أعلن! وأنا سأعلن انتقامي بعلامات الدخان الذي سيمحو

قراه ويسويها بالأرض.

كلاوديوس: قراه ستصبح قراك، سأجعلك زعيم الإقليم الجنوبي، سنعلنها الليلة. هل تدعني أوجهك؟

لايارتيس: أنا مصغ.

كلاوديوس: هاملت سيعود برفقة مجموعة من المنفيين والشيوعيين والحثالة الذين نبذهم الشعب منذ زمن. ويدعي أنه المخلص! لكي يحصل على دعم العامة سيلجأ للمسجد ليؤم الناس في صلاة الجمعة، ستواجهه هناك بألف من الرجال بثيابهم العسكرية – (تنفجر قنبلة على مقربة).

لايارتيس: و ما المقابل؟

كلاوديوس: ثلث الملك.

لايارتيس: ثلث لي وثلث لأبي.

كلاوديوس: النصف!

لايارتيس: اتفقنا، و إن كذبت عليّ، قتلتك.

(تدخل جيرترووד صارخة).

جيرتروود: شقيقتك، لايارتيس! جاءت إلى القصر مع غروب الشمس على قمم النخيل. وعيناها كوكبان متوهجان وثوبها ملئه الريح، ذهبت بإتجاهها وهي ترفع يدها كأنها تحيّي العالم، سقط زرّ من قميصها أتذكر ذلك الزر يا لايارتيس، وانحنيت لالتقاطه أثناء عودتي إلى القصر – كلا ! – عندما كنت هناك، اللحم الآدمي المتناثر والأوصال المتقطعة وجسدها كان كالينبوع اغتسلت منه: كم كان حارًا على وجهي، كم كانتا حارّتين رئتاها، وكم كانت حارّة أمعاؤها. لا أحد معفي، الإعفاء مستحيل. أنا أحمل ذنبي، أنا أحمله ...

لكن

لكن

لكن

هل ما زلت جميلة ؟

(تطفأ الأنوار)

الفصل الخامس

١ :

(عند مكتب أوفيليا، يضع الأعضاء ورودا. وتقام الصلوات الإسلامية).

(يدخل هاملت بثوب إسلامي قصير وبلحية طويلة).

هاملت: أحببتها .أحببتها حبا شريفاً.. (إلى لايارتيس) قتلته. قتلت أبيك و أبي. يمكنك الآن النظر إلي يا أمي أنـا الـذي قتلتـه فعلـت ذلك بدافع الحب. و ماذا يعني موت الأب، لايارتيس، ما الذي يعنيه حينما الهزيمة هي سر الميلاد ؟

جيرتروود: هاملت!

هاملت: إبك موت أبيك تحية للأحياء، ولا تبكيه تحية للملك! احتاجك معي في اعادة تشكيلُ هذه الأمة.

لايارتيس: أيها اللقيط !

هاملت: هل هذا هو الوفاء، لايارتيس؟ الوقوف إلى جوار الملك في مكان أبيك نفسه. أنت لست ظلا للموت، بل أنت الموت نفسه!

(لايارتيس يضرب هاملت على وجهه)

فليكن! والآن، هل نعد العدة ؟! من خيل، وسيف، ورباطة جأش!! وذكر لدخول الكوفة! فمعركة الجمل لا تزال قائمة !! أهكذا؟!

٢ :

(تاجر السلاح في مكتب هاملت)

تاجر السلاح: ليفخر بك أبوك.

هاملت : أبي قد مات. و أنت ما تزال هنا ؟

تاجر السلاح : أنا ذاهب. لقد انتهى دوري. أسعدتني خدمتك .

هاملت : ستندم عليها.

تاجر السلاح: أتترك الدار للأقدار تحكمها

والمجرمون لدفن الدار قد حضروا؟

هاملت : أخرج.

تاجر السلاح : سأنقل تحياتك لفورتنبراس .

هاملت: اخرج.

تاجر السلاح: وداعا يا صديقي.

هاملت: ارحل!

(يخرج تاجر السلاح)

٣ :

هاملت : من بوسعه النطق دون طاولات دون كراس دون نفاق، فلينطق

(صمت)

هذا الصمت سيوئدنا جميعا

(جرس بداية الجلسة)

مؤتمر هاملت

أشهد أن لا اله إلا اللّه وأن محمدا رسول اللّه.

أنا، هاملت، ابن هاملت، ابن هاملت الوريث الشرعي لعرش هذه الأمة حكمي سيكسر أصابع اللصوص، سيشل المنافقين، سيطفئ نيران الفسق المشتعلة في مدننا وسوف يعيد شعبنا النبيل إلى الصراط المستقيم. أعداؤنا لا يفهمون سوى لغة الدّم، لذا ولّى زمن القلم ودخلنا زمن السيف. لا تتظاهروا بالدهشة! فالعنف يولد الأمراء، والأمراء يولدون العنف، هذه هي لعنتنا. والمجد والخلود لشهدائنا الأبرار. (يصوتون)

جيرتروود : إلى أين هذا الجنون يا هاملت ... إلى أين ؟؟؟

هاملت : كفى من كلماتك يا أمي كفى فقد مل قلبي من هرائك واكتفى، وبات اللسان اضعف الأيمان و لا يتبقى لنا سوى أرواحنا. **(تصوت جيرتروود)**

(تم إعلان الحرب، أعمال غاضبة على المكاتب، طعن للملفات، وإتلاف للأوراق).

(يدخل مراسل الأمم المتحدة إلى مكتب كلاوديوس، يصدر له مذكّرة يتوجه إلى مكتب هاملت)

مراسل الأمم المتحدة : إن المجتمع الدولي ممثل بالأمم المتّحدة قد بعث لك بهذه الرسالة:

مفادها أنهم يستعدون لإرسال قوات حفظ السلام للمنطقة والإعداد لعقد مؤتمر قمة ترأسه رموز سياسية، لبحث الخلافات بين الأطراف المتنازعة.

هاملت : أدعو أسيادك إلى عرض خاص ليروا القتيل يرقص أمام قاتله عسى أن تعلموننا فنون الذبح وتبرئة الجاني!

مراسل الأمم المتحدة : ستقتل، هاملت. **(يخرج مراسل الأمم المتحدة)**

هاملت : لا، بل أسارع الخطى إلى حياة كريمة وخلود يعقب الموت.

مؤتمر هاملت

٤ :

كلاوديوس : إن التاريخ يعّد لنا أعظم تحد –

(يسمع تسجيل للكلمة ذاتها عبر مكبرات الصوت وكأنما دخل التاريخ وأقتحم اللحظة الآنية. ينهض كل عضو من على طاولته / طاولتها، يفتحون صندوق الذخيرة إلى جانبهم، يخرجون السلاح منها، ويتقدمون، مصغين بخوف وترقب. بينما يطفح سيل من التقارير الصحفية عن الأحداث التي تجري خارج أسوار غرفة المؤتمر. وعندما يسمعون إعلان موتهم، يسقطون، أمواتاً بكل بساطة وواقعية)

كلمة الرئيس كلاوديوس تملأ الشاشة

منذ ساعتين فقط، بدأت قواتنا هجومها على معاقل الإرهاب التابعة لهاملت وجيشه. والاشتباكات مازالت تتواصل حتى حين إلقاء هذه الكلمة. بدأ هذا الصراع عندما فرض هاملت حصارا على ديمقراطيتنا، وعلى قيمنا وشعبنا من خلال سلسلة أعمال وحشية من خطف وتفجيرات ارهابية تسببت في قتل العديد من الضحايا الأبرياء وهزّت المجتمع الدولي. والآن وقد استنفدت جميع المحاولات والجهود الممكنة في التوصّل إلى حل سلمي لا نجد أمامنا إلا خيار إرغامه على الخروج بالقوة – ولسوف ننجح في ذلك.

"هنا لندن" (النص التالي وهو التقرير الصحفي الذي يتداخل مع كلمة كلاوديوس عبر مكبرات الصوت)

التقرير الاعلامي : هنا لندن :

"اندلعت اليوم النيران في شوارع العاصمة، وانهارت المباني خلال هجوم ضار ومتواصل بواسطة طائرات أف – ١٦ التي مازالت موالية للملك. وفي هذه الأثناء، ينتشر ولي العهد هاملت، قائد جبهة التحرير مع جنوده البالغ عددهم خمسة آلاف جندي، على طول مركز المدينة.

كلاوديوس : وبينما أتحدث لكم هنا، تشق طائراتنا طريقها ضد أهداف عسكرية داخل المدينة حيث يستخدم هاملت وأتباعه المباني المدنية، المستشفيات، والمدارس كمأوى.

التقرير الاعلامي : وفي أنباء غير مؤكدة، ذكر أن الملكة جيرتروود لقيت مصرعها أثناء محاولتها منع دبابات الملك من تطويق إبنها المحاصر داخل المسجد الكبير

(تسقط جيرترووود)

كلاوديوس : قد يتسائل البعض لماذا نضرب الآن؟ لما لا ننتظر؟ والجواب واضح: العالم لم يعد بامكانه الإنتظار أكثر.

التقرير الاعلامي : وأفادت التقارير الواردة في ١٠ صباحاً أن لايارتيس أصيب بنيران مدفعية هاون ووصفت حالته بالحرجة

(يسقط لايارتيس).

كلاوديوس : كنت آمل عند إتخاذنا القرار بنفيه في المناظرة التاريخية، أن نضع حداً لحياته الإجرامية، ولكن تبين إني كنت مخطئاً، واليوم سيشهد العالم تصحيح ذلك الخطأ.

(يسقط كلاوديوس)

هاملت (يائساً) : باسمك اللهم

اختلقت لعنة

لأسطر تاريخ الآخرين

بدماء شعبي

ولربما أصعب الأشياء

أن نجد العزم لنستيقظ صباحاً

لنتلمس بين الأطلال درباً

إن إكتشاف الحقيقة بعد فوات الأوان

لهو الجحيم

(يسقط هاملت).   (يدخل فورتنبراس بين الجثث.)

فورتنبــراس: براز وأحشـاء وعرق، أمـوات البشـر فقط يمكن أن تكون رائحتهم هكذا. لـدي ادعاءات ومطالبات بموجب كتب سـماوية بهذه الأرض، فهي فارغة وقاحلة ووجودي بهـا حقيقة ليسـت محض خيـال. لـن يكون ذلك سـهلا ، فالإرهاب لم يهـزم بعد، سيموت الكبار ولسوف ينسى الصغار وسـتزهر هـذه الأرض .ما نراه هنـا لن يحدث لنا قط.

هذا هـو الفجـر ومولد...

(صوت عال ومشوش عبر مكبرات الصوت، تقطع لفظ الكلمة الآتية بحيث لا يستطيع إلا لفظ مطلعها)

از...

از...

از...

بمسـاعدتكم سـيكون المسـتقبل مشرقاً. فلتصوب الدبّابات إلى الغـرب، وليؤد القـادة التحية العسكرية.

(تطفأ الأضواء ببطء مع دخول تاجر السلاح)

ستارة النهايـة

سليمان البسام

(٢٠٠٢ – ٢٠٠٤)